Captain Psychology's
101 Questions About the Brain

Dr. Ken Tangen

ISBN-10:1722227451
ISBN-13:9781722227456

DEDICATION

To my teachers.
I can never repay their knowledge, wisdom and kindness. Special thanks to Dr. Myrthalene Thompson, who introduced me to physiological psychology, taught me to not be a fussy-headed thinker, and showed me that psychology could be more than talk therapy.

CONTENTS

Vision

Other Senses

Memory

ACKNOWLEDGMENTS

The brain is a complicated topic, and I'm sure I have gotten some things wrong (I just don't know which ones they are). The errors are all mine but thanks to the work of Jeremy McCollum, Katrina Tangen and all who reviewed early drafts of the manuscript, there are a lot less errors than there would have been without their input. Thanks, gang.

101
Questions
?

1. What Is the Brain?

Surprisingly, there are three definitions of the brain. Most people think of the nearly three-pound chunk of gray matter in the head. This is an excellent choice. The cerebrum processes information, integrates sensations, plans activities and coordinates activities.

A more generous definition of the brain is to include the cerebrum, the cerebellum, and the brainstem. This definition is a better description of how the brain operates. It is a system of interacting parts, all working at the same time.

An even more extensive definition of the brain is everything in the head. This includes the cerebrum, cerebellum, brain stem, basal ganglia, the thalamus system, the limbic system, and everything else needed for the brain to function.

2. How Is the Brain Like A Pizza?

Think of the brain as a super-computer laid out on a giant foldable circuit board. It is always active (even when you sleep) and constantly interacts with the super-computer in the other cerebral hemisphere. Two super-computers created from two large pizzas.

Each cerebral hemisphere is about the size of a large pizza that has been folded many times. To make a hemisphere of the brain, you take a bunch of neurons (50 billion or so) and form them into a ball of dough. Then roll it out until it is about an eighth of an inch thick. Then fold it, refold it, re-refold it…repeated, until it is about the size of a grapefruit. Then flatten it out a bit and stuff it into the skull. Now do the same for the other hemisphere.

3. How Is the Brain Like A Fist?

Each hemisphere, when complete, looks like a fist. The main portion of the fist (from the knuckles forward) is the frontal lobe. This is the largest segment. In the brain, it is separated from the parietal lobe by the central sulcus (groove) and from the temporal lobe by the lateral sulcus.

The frontal lobe has three major regions. One controls your movements (motor cortex), one plans your movements (pre-motor cortex) and one makes distinctions and rules (prefrontal cortex). If you are deciding or doing, you're using your frontal lobe.

The knuckles are the parietal lobe. It is located under the parietal bone. The parietal lobe is important for processing language processing, giving you a 3-D view of the world, and helping you know where you are in relation to everything else. It also processes touch, pain, and temperature information.

The back of your fist is the occipital lobe. It is the primary processor of vision. There is a direct one-to-one mapping of the retinal image and specialized cells for analyzing color and motion.

The thumb of your fist is the temporal lobe. It processes sound, language, and visual memories. Some believe the left temporal lobe stores semantic memory (your internal dictionary and encyclopedia), and that the right sides stores episodic memory (stories of your life). It is probably more complicated than that.

4. How Big Is the Brain?

The easiest way to measure brain size is to measure its outside dimensions. An adult brain about six inches long, five and a half inches wide and nearly 4 inches tall.

In terms of how many neurons are in the brain, no one really knows. It is impossible to get an accurate count. Estimates are that the cerebral cortex has 86-100 billion neurons. About 25% of them are gray matter neurons (unmyelinated).

Weighing the brain is another approach. A newborn's brain is about three-quarters of a pound (350-400 grams). An adult's brain is about 3 pounds(1300-1400 grams), pound and a half for each hemisphere.

Men have heavier brains (by about 100 grams), with larger regions for spatial relations and emotional responses (parietal lobe and amygdala, respectively). Women have more developed frontal regions for emotional regulation.

5. Is the Brain Really Gray?

Pretty much. At least it starts off that way. Neurons are inherently brownish-gray or grayish-brown. It's not pure gray but that is the overall impression. This is the way the brain starts out. It is a collection of "gray matter."

Gradually many of the brain's neurons become wrapped in a fatty substance called myelin. Myelin insulates the neurons so they don't unintentionally trigger each other. It also increases their transmission speed, making them more efficient. The fatty nature of myelin makes the covered neurons look white, so it is called "white matter." Eventually, at about age 30, you end up with an outer layer of gray and an inner core of white.

6. Is the Brain Smooth?

The brain starts out smooth. At about the 12th week of development, the fetal brain begins to thicken and grow rapidly. As it grows, the cortex remains thin but more folds are created, producing more overall surface area. Unencumbered by myelin, gray matter grows faster than white matter, making the ridges bulge out and the grooves deepen. A groove is a sulcus, and a ridge is a gyrus.

Rare genetic conditions can lead to inadequate brain development, including not enough brain folds (lissencephalies), too many brain folds (polymicrogyria), and brain folds that are too thick (pachygyria).

7. Are There Four or Six Lobes?

It depends. There are four major lobes: occipital, temporal, parietal and frontal. There are two minor bulges (lobes): limbic and insular.

Lobe means bulge or segment (like leaves of a tree). It is an anatomical distinction, not functional. Moving your hand to pick up a bottle of water involves portions of all the brain's lobes. But each region has its specialties.

The other two lobes (lobettes?) are tucked inside. The limbic lobe is a small arched region where the frontal, parietal and temporal lobes meet. There is no agreed-upon list of what is included. The fusiform gyrus is usually described as part of the temporal lobe's bottom edge but some include it in the limbic lobe. Similarly, the hippocampus is a semicircular structure that passes through the temporal and frontal lobes. Some include it in the limbic lobe; some think of it as its own structure. With all this definitional confusion, you can see why you've never heard of the limbic lobe.

The insular cortex is where your thumb connects to the rest of your fist, hidden inside the groove there. It is involved in perception, self-awareness, cognition, emotion, and consciousness. Since it is a combination of the frontal, parietal and temporal lobes, think of it as an integrator of these regions. This region can also be referred to as the temporoparietal junction.

8. What Does the Occipital Lobe Do?

If the brain is a fist, the occipital lobe is back of your hand. Although the occipital lobe is the smallest lobe, it accounts for nearly 20% of the brain's activity. It is a busy place. It is the primary processing center for vision, our most used sense. Vision is an essential part of object identification, moving, hunting and gathering. Vision is a big deal. But that is not the occipital lobe's only function. The occipital lobe is also involved in reading, visualization, and alpha waves.

When you read a story which contains no pictures, you use the occipital lobe. The same centers that see real external scenes are used to generate internal images of fictional scenes. You generate "visual" images when a book describes a scene. You feel like you're there with the hero because you can "see" what is happening.

Similarly, when you visualize how a creation will look, you use the occipital lobe. It doesn't do it alone. Other parts of the brain are involved. But mental images are "seen" by our "mind's eye." This seeing process is probably a combination of three theories. Paivio's dual-code theory suggests that we represent things both as images and as word descriptions. Images work well for objects and concrete ideas. Words work better for abstract concepts. But it is also true that we are meaning extractors. We don't store images or details, we symbolically store meanings (propositional theory). And, whenever we visualize, we use the same systems as we do in real life (functional-equivalency theory). We visualize with the occipital lobe, visualize movements with the motor cortex, and experience remembered smells in our olfactory system. We don't have a specialized mental representation system; we use the systems we already have.

The occipital lobes do more than vision and visualization. They emit alpha brain waves. Alphas occur when our eyes are closed. When we are wide awake, we emit beta waves. Beta waves are uncoordinated rapid waves, indicating that different parts of the brain are all doing their own thing at the same time. When we close our eyes and relax, we emit alpha waves, which are slower and more coordinated than beta waves. The alpha waves are initiated by the thalamus but radiate out of the occipital lobe when our eyes are closed. If open our eyes, no matter how relaxed we are, the alpha waves stop.

Alpha waves that occur during REM sleep radiate from the frontal lobes. Why do alpha waves occur during REM? Don't know. Some think it is a good thing (providing a semi-wakeful period). Others think it interferes with restful sleep (alpha wave intrusion). People with chronic disabilities (chronic fatigue syndrome, major depression, fibromyalgia, etc.) often have this intrusion but its effects aren't clear.

9. What Does the Temporal Lobe Do?

If the brain is a fist, the temporal lobe is your thumb. It is the second largest lobe and is involved in many processes. Think of the temporal lobe as a 3-story building. The bottom floor is devoted to object and face recognition. This is the fusiform gyrus. It receives input for the occipital lobe (the ventral or what stream). Its job is to figure out what you are looking at.

The middle floor is devoted to memory. This is the hippocampus and adjacent temporal areas. It is involved in visual memory, identifying familiar smells, and transferring memories from temporary usage (working memory) to permanent storage (long-term memory). The hippocampus isn't involved in retrieving things from long-term memory, just putting them in. It also helps store and encodes spatial information, and how to get from one place to another (cognitive maps).

The top floor specializes in sound, language, and music. It is the primary projection area for sound perception and is organized in concentric circles. The primary motor cortex is surrounded by the regions which further process sounds, words and phrases.

10. What Does the Parietal Lobe Do?

The parietal lobe is a multi-function region at the top-back of the head. If you have a bald spot or a hair swirl, you know where the parietal lobe is. Inside, it is stuck between the frontal lobe and the occipital lobe. The parietal lobe is the third-largest or second-smallest lobe, depending on your view. It is larger than the occipital lobe but smaller than the temporal and frontal lobes.

Here are some of the things the parietal lobe is involved in: counting, physical navigation, 2-point discrimination, touch localization, reading long passages, object manipulation, holding a gaze, remembering what you're saying, dyslexia, apraxia, relationships between numbers, spatial orientation, getting dressed, imagery, and understanding symbols. Like the occipital lobe, all of the parietal lobe's functions are automatic and not under conscious control.

The parietal lobe processes visual information it receives from the occipital lobe (the dorsal stream). It uses this information and other inputs to provide a 3-D view of your environment. This helps you know where things are and how to reach them. Data from the occipital lobe is compared to data obtained directly from the optic chiasm and superior colliculus. You get fast response to moving objects, quick visualization of targets (target detection), and a clear, if slower, understanding of where everything is.

It processes pain, temperature and pressure information. Temperature and pain information is routed to the parietal lobe but it is less clear how this information is organized and processed. Touch information is clearly mapped but pain isn't. Pain also involves the frontal lobe for determining context and significance. The parietal lobe integrates and interprets sensory information, everything but smell.

Anatomically, the parietal lobe is located under the parietal bone. It is organized into three regions, one in front of the other. Think of them as a three-room apartment.

First, the front room integrates all of the sensory information. It is organized like a homunculus (a distorted map of the body). The body has two of these maps. One, in the frontal lobe, is for motor movement. The other, in the parietal lobe, is for sensory input. Both maps are quite similar, with large areas devoted to the hands, lips, and face.

Like the homunculus in the motor cortex of the frontal lobe, there is an inverse relationship between body location and cortical location. Input from the toes is on the top of the head. As you move down the cortex, you encounter body regions higher in the body (leg, hands, and face). Surprisingly, the face is upside right. The forehead, eyes, nose, mouth, and jaw are represented in that order top to bottom in the cortical map.

Second, the intraparietal region (stuck between the other regions) passes things back and forth, coordinates hand movements, and processes the location, size, and shape of targets within your reach.

Third, at the back, the posterior parietal lobe processes the visual information it receives from the occipital lobe. This region is gaze-centered and remaps itself every time you look in a new direction.

11. What Does the Frontal Lobe Do?

The frontal lobe of the cerebral cortex is divided into three parts. The first region is the motor cortex, which is located at the back of the frontal lobe. It controls voluntary movement and is organized in homunculus fashion (feet at the top, tongue at the bottom). Trigger the appropriate spot and that portion of the body will move. The motor cortex is sometimes called M1. The motor cortex is involved in the execution of movements.

The second part is just in front of the motor cortex. It includes the prefrontal cortex and the supplemental cortex. Together these regions are involved in the planning and coordination of movements.

The third area and the largest is the prefrontal cortex. It is involved in thinking, deciding, and choosing. The prefrontal cortex has three regions: dorsolateral, orbitofrontal and ventromedial.

12. What Does the Motor Cortex Do?

Movement is complicated. Even simple movement involves many regions of the brain. Like most things, the brain uses several regions to initiate movements. There are areas for processing sensory information, selecting targets, and the planning, preparation, sequencing and executing movements.

The top five components of the motor cortex include three regions in the frontal lobe and two in the parietal lobe. First, the posterior parietal cortex integrates sensory information and converts it into motor commands. It has some part in motor planning but mostly it is in responsible for issuing "do this" commands to the rest of the motor cortex.

Second, the primary somatosensory cortex is between the posterior parietal cortex and the frontal lobe. Functionally, it can be considered a part of both lobes. It integrates sensory information but is also part of the motor cortex circuitry. This region is organized in a homunculus-like fashion, giving an orderly representation of what is being touched on the other side of the body. The left somatosensory cortex receives information from the right side of the body; the right represents tactile information from the left side of the body. Large regions are devoted to reporting touching of the lips and hands, less area is devoted to legs and arms.

Third, the primary motor cortex (sometimes called M1) is located in the rear portion of the frontal lobe. It is involved in the execution of voluntary movements by sending signals to the spine and onto the muscles. The primary motor cortex carries out the instructions given by the rest of the motor cortex. It, like the somatosensory cortex, is organized in a homunculus fashion (feet at the top, tongue at the bottom).

Fourth, the premotor cortex is in front of the primary motor cortex. It, and the supplemental motor cortex (fifth) deserves a more detailed description.

13. What Does the Premotor Cortex Do?

Australian neurologist Alfred Walter Campbell was the first to differentiate between the primary motor cortex and the premotor cortex. The primary motor cortex contains Betz cells (large-bodied cells with long axons that connect the brain to the spine). The premotor cortex looks different under a microscope. It acts as an intermediate step between planning and execution.

The premotor cortex can be divided into four regions: up, down, frontal and back. The front portion (rostral) of the dorsal cortex (upper) seems to be involved in associating external sensory stimuli with movements. In essence, it is learning rules about how to respond to different stimulus conditions. The back portion (caudal) of the dorsal cortex helps guide reach movements. When you pick up a glass of water, this portion helps control that action.

The front portion (dorsal) of the lower section (ventral) is needed for grasping and moving your hands to your mouth. This is also the region where mirror neurons were first discovered. The back portion of the lower section reacts to objects in your peri-personal space (items close to or headed toward your body). They appear to be part of your early-warning system of incoming sights, sounds, and touch.

Together, the four parts of the premotor cortex take instructions from the higher level planning regions and prepare plans of attack. If the prefrontal cortex houses the generals, the field commanders are in the premotor cortex.

14. What Does the Supplementary Motor Cortex Do?

The supplemental motor cortex (or supplementary, if you prefer) helps plan movements, particularly sequences of movements. It also is involved in coordinating and executing movements requiring both sides of the body.

This region is not easily mapped. It projects directly to the spine but there are lots of overlapping influences. Each neuron seems to influence many other neurons and muscles. There are two supplementary motor cortexes (one in each hemisphere) but each one influences neurons on both sides of the body. It is not clear if one hemisphere plans movements for both sides or if they each generate their own plan.

Mirror neurons are located in the supplementary motor cortex (plus several other premotor regions). They are neurons that fire when you do a specific task and when you watch someone else do that same task. Part of the preparing to execute a movement is accessing routines that have worked before or that you have seen others do.

15. What Does the Prefrontal Cortex Do?

If there is a center of personality and thinking, it is the front of the frontal lobe: the prefrontal cortex. This region is responsible for executive functions, such as predicting outcomes, comparing expected and actual values, and the suppression and control of social interactions.

There are three subdivisions to the prefrontal cortex. The dorsolateral division is involved in working memory, rule management, and higher-order reasoning. The orbitofrontal cortex is also involved in executive functions and cognitive flexibility. It is located just above the eyes. The ventromedial cortex is involved in motivation, empathy, and resource allocation.

16. What Is the Dorsolateral Cortex?

The dorsolateral region is in the prefrontal cortex of the frontal lobe. It is the last part of the brain to be myelinated. It is still developing at 30 years of age. This region interacts with other parts of the brain and houses the rules about rules. It is involved in high-level planning, spatial information, integration of sensory information, and executive processes. If damaged, there is impaired social judgment, difficulty with abstract thinking, and problems with working memory. Tumors here produce symptoms similar to schizophrenia. When you suffer from sleep deprivation, this is the region of the brain impacted.

It keeps rules about rules, and supervises/interacts with the other two divisions. It is the last part of the brain to myelinate, so it is still developing until you are about 30 years old. Sleep deprivation impacts this region, making it hard to concentrate. You feel disoriented, and your thinking is fuzzy. Damage to this region produces impaired thinking, loss of working memory, and symptoms that are similar to schizophrenia.

17. What Is the Orbitofrontal Cortex?

The orbitofrontal region is below the dorsolateral cortex. Named for its location above the eyes (orbits), this cortex is one of the least explored and least understood regions of the brain. Exploring with MRIs or other imaging systems is difficult because the tissue is so close to the sinuses. The contrast between the tissue and the air-filled sinuses make it is difficult to get a clear picture. Most of our understanding is based on a functional analysis of what the regions do, and not on how it is organized.

The orbitofrontal region is involved in personal responsibility, mood, drive, and cognitive processing. It houses decision-making rules and intuitive judgments. When your gut is talking to you, it's your orbitofrontal region. This area tracks expectations of reward and punishment. It compares the expected outcome with actual outcomes.

The orbitofrontal cortex has extensive reciprocal connections with other brain regions. It both sends and receives inputs from most aspects of the brain and limbic system. Both the ventral and dorsal visual streams project to this area. It uses these inputs to assess the affective value of reinforcers, and to control complex activities such as social adjustment, personal responsibility, motivation, and mood.

Although the orbitofrontal region is associated with many disorders, including ADHD and OCD, there are three key conditions to remember: Alzheimer's, gambling and drug addiction.

Alzheimer's. The orbitofrontal cortex and the hippocampus are among the first areas to show Alzheimer's tangles. The tangles are neurons whose axons collapse, getting tangled up in themselves and unable to fire.

Gambling.

The orbitofrontal cortex is involved in evaluating rewards and regulating personal responsibility. Damage here makes it impossible to control impulses (push "Don't Push Button") or to change rules, even when you know the rule isn't working well. They are like three-year-olds who learn the shape game (rabbits on the left, boats on the right) but can't change to the color game (red rabbits and boats on the left, blue rabbits and boats on the right). They understand the rule, can follow the rule if it is the first one presented but can't change to a different rule.

The third disorder which seems to be caused by damage to the orbitofrontal region is drug addiction. Drug abuse damages this area's ability to control decisions. People have less free will. There is an increased motivation to take a drug. Activity here is proportional to the level of drug craving. Prolonged withdrawal shows lower levels of activity here compared to normal subjects. Lesions here cause similar symptoms to drug addiction: problems with decision-making, emotional regulation, and impulsivity.

Anatomically, there is no separation between the orbitofrontal and ventromedial regions. The distinction is simply based on connections and functional processing.

18. What Is the Ventromedial Cortex?

The ventromedial cortex is anatomically inseparable from the orbitofrontal cortex, but it has different inputs and outputs. Like the orbitofrontal cortex, this region has direct connections to the amygdala and the basal ganglia. It is involved in cognitive flexibility, thinking, and executive processes. But the ventromedial cortex seems to specialize in processing empathy, emotional salience, and motivational information. It estimates how much effort is required to complete a given task. Damage here decreases your ability to assess risk, make decisions and control emotions.

The ventromedial region is involved in empathy, emotional salience, and top-down and bottom-up processing. It assesses motivational information and estimates how much effort is required to complete a task. The ventromedial region is activated by conflict and inconsistencies. It functions as an error detector and central distributor.

When it detects incompatible stimuli, it evaluates and assigns its resolution to another portion of the brain. It then monitors progress and suggests appropriate actions. It houses rules about rewards, error detection, emotional cues, and pain. Damage here may help explain schizophrenia, social anxiety, and ADHD.

19. What's Actually in The Brain?

The brain is composed of neurons, glial cells, and blood vessels.

The neurons in the brain are generally rather small. They typically don't have long axons because they don't have that far to travel. They are surrounded by other neurons, so they often don't need long axons. One exception: Purkinje neurons. These neurons connect the motor cortex (on top of the brain) to the spinal cord. When you want to move your fingers, you want a fast connection between brain and muscles. Purkinje neurons have large cell bodies (think large battery pack) and long axons (for quick connections to motor neurons).

Glial cells are support cells. They hold things in place, help reuptake neurotransmitters, and generally run the place. They supply oxygen, prevent crossfirings, and act as the brain's immune system. There are about the same number of glial cells as neurons (85-86 billion).

Blood vessels take blood from the heart and bring it to the brain. The carotid arteries run up the sides of the neck and deliver blood to the front of the brain. The vertebral arteries go up the back of the neck, connect at the circle of Willis, and supply blood to the back of the brain and the cerebellum.

20. What Are Neurons?

A neuron is a single cell that acts like a little battery. It is composed of a soma (cell body), several dendrites (thick, bumpy outgrowths) and one axon (long, thin extension). The dendrites have receptors that bind to chemicals floating in extracellular space. The chemicals (called neurotransmitters) bind to the receptors causing a change in the cell's electrical potential (making the neuron more or less likely to fire). When the electrical potential for a neuron reaches or passes its threshold (which is different for each cell), an impulse travels down the axon until it reaches the end, where its own neurotransmitter is stored and released.

In the brain and spinal cord, collections of neurons are called nuclei. In the rest of the body, they are called ganglia. In the brain and spinal cord, collections of axons are called tracts. In the rest of the body, they are called nerves.

21. How Many Neurons Are in The Brain?

Lots.

There are probably about 100 billion neurons. But it is difficult to know for sure. There is no easy way to count them. You should also know that there are trillions of glial and support cells in the brain. Neurons are not alone.

22. What Is a Neuron's Anatomy?

Like any other cell, there is a nucleus for storing DNA, RNA, mitochondria and other structures and processes needed to keep the cell alive. In a small neuron, the soma, axon, and dendrites are the main structures. In larger neurons, there might be an axon hillock (a buildup where the axon attaches to the soma). In any case, the axon will have an initial segment (area closest to the soma) where many voltage-gated sodium channels reside.

At the end of the axon, vesicles store neurotransmitters (usually only one neurotransmitter per neuron) and terminal buttons release the neurotransmitter through the cell's membrane. A structure of tubes (the endoplasmic reticulum) gives structural support to the axon. These tubes carry supplies out from the soma and bring waste back. One of the problems with Alzheimer's is that the endoplasmic reticulum breaks apart, allowing the axon to get tangled up in itself.

23. Why Do Neurons Fire?

Two reasons: neurotransmitters and gap junctions. A typical neuron is activated when another neuron releases a neurotransmitter. When the neurotransmitter binds to the receptors on the dendrites, ligand-gated sodium channels open (allowing sodium in and making the cell more positive). If enough neurotransmitter binds to enough receptors and enough protein-gated (ligand-gated) sodium channels open, the voltage inside the cell will rise past its threshold, triggering the voltage-gated channels to open.

Voltage-gated channels open in sequence. Think of them as a series of thermometers in a row. If the first gate opens, it lets in sodium, which makes the region around the next gate more positive, making it open. Like a series of dominos, the opening of each gate triggers the next gate to open. The impulse (series of gates opening) travels down the axon.

The second way neurons are triggered is voltage. If the axons of two neurons are too close together, the sequential firing along one axon can trigger the other axon to be activated too. These axon to axon connections are called gap junctions.

24. Why Is Sodium So Important?

Sodium ions are positively charged and unable to enter a negatively-charged neuron until a gate opens and allows them in. There are three reasons sodium channel gates open.

First, a neurotransmitter binds to a receptor on a dendrite. This chemical bond triggers ligand-gated channels to open. These channels only open when a neurotransmitter connects to a receptor. The result is a small increase in the amount of sodium in the neural cell, making it more likely to fire.

Second, a neuron's internal voltage rises to a preset threshold. When a portion of a neuron reaches about -55 mvlts. (in most neurons), the sodium channel in that region will open. These voltage-gated channels respond to the internal voltage at their location like a furnace thermostat. There is no great thinking involved. If a threshold is met, the thermostat (or sodium gate) will be activated.

These two types of sodium gate openings produce ionotropic effects. That is, they have a localized effect on gates that will allow sodium ions to enter the cell. This is the most common way neurons are activated. It is either by a neurotransmitter-gated or a voltage-gated channel.

The third reason sodium gates open is as part of a widespread process that impacts many cells. These are called metabotropic effects, and are the result of activating a g-protein. G-proteins change their shape and basically stick their foot in a sodium gate, preventing it from immediately closing. But this need not be a localized effect. G-proteins often impact many cells at once.

25. How Fast Do Neural Signals Travel?

Neurons vary in thickness, speed, and insulation. The thicker they are, the faster they are and the more insulation they have.

A-Alpha neurons are the thickest neurons and have the most insulation (myelination). This combination of thickness and myelin allows these neurons to send signals at 265 miles per hour. They are great for controlling muscle movements and returning proprioceptive stimuli about where your arms and legs are located. If you stub your toe, the A-Alphas notify the brain your foot has moved.

A-Beta neurons are the second thickest. They are myelinated and send signals at 165 mph. The A-Betas notify the brain that your toe and an object have collided. They send sensory information to the brain.

A-Delta neurons are the smallest myelinated neurons. Their signals travel at 75 miles per hour. They signal the sharp pain of tissue damage.

C fibers are the thinnest sensory neurons. They are not myelinated and their signals travel at 2 mph. They signal chronic and dull pain.

26. What Are Neurotransmitters?

This is a class of chemicals that facilitate the firing of neurons. Synthesized and stored inside a neuron, a neurotransmitter is released from one neuron, diffuses across extracellular space and binds to one or more other neurons. The binding of the neurotransmitter to the receptors on a dendrite impacts the likelihood of the post-synaptic neuron firing.

There are over 100 neurotransmitters (also called chemical messengers) in the brain. The most common are glutamate (an exciter) and GABA (an inhibitor).

27. What Is A Synapse?

A synapse is a donut hole. It is not a structure. It is the space between structures. A synapse is the space between neurons. It is usually about 30 nm wide, but varies.

Synapse is from the Greek synapsis, meaning connection or conjoining. Neurons with only one or two synapses send signals quickly. You have a motor neuron in your spine which has a long axon down to your big toe. It is about 3 feet long and doesn't synapse along the way. Single neurons are like express elevators, while a series of neurons and synapses is like stopping at every floor. Every synapse slows the signal down a bit.

28. What Are Glial Cells?

Glial cells (neuroglia) provide the support system for neurons. There are many subtypes, each with their own specialties. Some glia produce myelin to insulate neurons from each other. Some, like astrocytes, hold neurons in place, aid in the reuptake of neurotransmitters and signal each other. Macroglia are large cells that structurally help hold the brain together. Damage to macroglia destroys the blood-brain barrier and makes it difficult for the brain to repair itself. Damage to microglia (small glial cells) or malfunctioning microglia is associated with Alzheimer's, Parkinson's and ALS.

29. What Are Myelinating Glial Cells?

Glial cells are support cells that insulate neurons from each other, allowing for faster transmission and let interference. There are two types of myelinating glial cells. In the brain, myelin is produced by oligodendrocytes. They sort of look like blobs with straws (axons) sticking through them but never touching each other.

In the peripheral system, the work is done by myelinating Schwann cells (as opposed to the non-myelinating Schwann cells). The myelinating Schwann cell wraps around an axon, like a ring on a finger. Layer after layer forms until the myelin coating is quite thick. In long axons, multiple rings of myelinating Schwann cells will cover an axon, with small gaps between them. These gaps are the nodes of Ranvier, and act as superchargers, making the neural impulse faster.

30. How Are the Brain's Capillaries Different?

Blood flows from large arteries to small blood vessels to capillaries. In other parts of the body, the walls of these capillaries are rather loosely constructed, allowing even rather large molecules to pass from the blood to the surrounding cells. This allows bacteria, viruses, drugs, immune system killer cells and most everything else to cross back and forth into and out of the blood system. Our immune system uses the same blood supply to find and kill any troublesome diseases, to the best of its ability.

In the brain, the big arteries and blood vessels are as leaky as in the rest of the body. But the capillaries are different. Their walls are very tightly constructed, allowing only very small molecules to get out. Oxygen and carbon dioxide easily pass through in either direction. But almost everything else is stuck in the capillary and can't easily get out.

In addition to tighter internal construction, brain capillaries also have outside support. Several proteins connect sections of the capillary walls side by side so the tight junctions are sort of glued together. Pericytes are contracting cells that cover the capillaries like shrink wrap. A final layer is composed of the feet of astrocytes which weigh and hold everything in place.

This provides a very stable environment. Together the components of the blood-brain barrier provide a diffusion barrier between the blood and brain cells. Aside from oxygen and carbon dioxide, everything else must be transported across, like a ferry boat.

When the blood-brain barrier is intact, not infected and not leaking, it works surprisingly well. It keeps out all large molecules and nearly all small molecules. This is both the good news and the bad news. Most bad stuff can't get into the brain: good news. But most medicines can't get through either. Once infected, there is little that can be done to treat brain diseases.

31. Is the Blood-Brain Barrier Like A Plastic Sack?

The brain doesn't have much of an immune system to protect it. It mostly relies on isolation. The blood-brain barrier (BBB) keeps disease out of the brain but it is not as much of a barrier as it sounds. It is not a membrane or sack. It is not tissue or bone. The blood-brain barrier is composed of the blood vessels in the brain. It is how the small capillaries in the brain are constructed. Being "inside" the blood-brain barrier depends on the tightness of the capillaries. Tissue beside a tight capillary is "in" but tissue next to a capillary whose walls have been pushed apart by high blood pressure is effectively "out." Being inside or outside varies across regions of the brain, making it a rather arbitrary distinction.

32. What Endangers The BBB?

The barrier is a living structure which changes with its environment. The higher the blood pressure, the harder it is for the astrocyte-covered capillaries to hold together. Prolonged high blood pressure breaks down the tight-junctions of the blood-brain barrier, making the brain more susceptible to toxins and infections.

When you have an infection, the BBB relaxes a bit. With most infections, no great harm occurs. It is a temporary matter. When the meninges (the tri-layer structure that separates the brain from the skull) gets infected, the blood-brain barrier is more permanently compromised, causing meningitis.

In addition to meningitis, an infection elsewhere in the body can be carried by the blood to the brain where it might take advantage of weaknesses in the blood-brain barrier. Systemic infections or compromised immune systems might also attack the blood-brain barrier. There is a tie between BBB damage and epilepsy. Albumin (a protein commonly in the blood) seems to interact negatively with astrocytes.

In MS, there is an infection or the immune system thinks/perceives that there is an infection. In defense, a large number of white blood cells are generated. Some of these T lymphocytes appear to cross a compromised blood-brain barrier, enter the brain, and attack the myelin (disrupting neural signals). Similarly, in neuromyelitis optica, (a rare condition) antibodies appear to cross the blood-brain barrier and attack the aquaporin 4 protein (needed for astrocyte feet). And Alzheimer's disease allows amyloid beta to enter through the BBB, covering and overwhelming the astrocytes, until they die.

You can be born with or acquire structural problems too. The mutated Huntington protein, a result of Huntington's disease, makes it more difficult to form new blood vessels, and makes the ones which are formed leaky.

33. What Are Brain Waves?

The brain is filled with billions of neurons, each acting like a tiny battery which periodically discharges its voltage. One neuron firing would look like a single spike in voltage. Several neurons firing in a sequence is a spike train, like dominoes knocking each other over. Multiple spike trains form regional patterns. Many neurons, spike trains and regions firing at the same time form complex patterns.

If each neuron fired independently, the overall pattern of activity would be random. But because the brain's neurons often fire in sequences, the overall pattern can be observed and measured. These patterns of oscillating neural activity are called brain waves.

34. What Is Amplitude, Phase & Frequency?

Brain waves vary in amplitude, frequency, and phase. Phase indicates whether a neuron or neural circuit is firing or resetting itself. Although phase information can be useful for describing individual neurons, phase information isn't that useful when looking at overall brain activity because they cancel each other out.

Amplitude is how much voltage is involved. Oddly, when you're awake your amplitudes are small. The larger amplitude waves come when you are asleep.

Frequency is how often the firing occurs. As it turns out, amplitude and frequency seem to be negatively correlated. The higher the amplitude, the slower the waves. We have low amplitude but frequent firings when we are awake. When we are asleep, the brain fires less often but with bigger spikes.

35. What Are the Four Main Types of Brain Waves?

Right now, you are awake and your brain is doing several things at once. There is no synchronicity in the pattern; every region is doing its own thing. This firing pattern is called beta wave activity. Beta waves are low amplitude waves (5-10 microvolts) that occur 12-30 times per second. Beta waves are like the choppy waves in the bay.

When you close your eyes to relax, you exhibit alpha waves. These are slower in frequency (8-12 per second) but larger (30-200 microvolts) and more synchronized across the brain. Alpha waves are like rolling ocean waves.

Theta waves occur in the transition during sleep from alpha waves to delta waves. They are slower in frequency (4-8 per second) but at the high end of amplitude for beta waves (10 microvolts). You use beta when awake, alpha when relaxed, and theta when daydreaming.

When you're in deep sleep, you have more and more delta waves. They are the slowest brain waves (2-4 cycles per second) and have the highest voltage peaks (20-200 microvolts) You can't get much slower than two cycles; one is very slow and zero means you're brain dead. Delta waves are about as low as you can get.

These are the main four main brain waves. There are some others you might hear about. Gamma waves are high-frequency waves at about 40 Hz (cycles per second). They may have something to do with consciousness but are mostly still a mystery. The other oddity are the Mu waves. At 8-12 Hz, they are similar to alpha waves but might have something to do with mirror neurons.

36. Why Are There Two Brain Halves?

Everyone who has a backbone (vertebrates) has a brain with a left and a right side. There is a basic building plan used to make reptiles, rodents, amphibians, fish, birds, four4-footed friends, and humans. It starts with one cell and subdivides into two cells, always creating symmetrical structures. If you get a left leg, you get a right one. If you get a left eye, you get a right one. If you get a left brain, you get a right one.

The bilateral symmetry results in symmetrical animals: an equal number of objects on each side. If you're a flounder or other flat fish, your eyes might migrate to one side but they were originally symmetrical.

37. How Are the Hemispheres Different?

The hemispheres aren't identical. They are fractured mirror images. The right hemisphere is slightly warped, located a bit forward and is a bit smaller (by about 100-200 million neurons). There tends to be more norepinephrine used by the right hemisphere, (more dopamine used in the left), and more white matter on the right (more gray matter in the left hemisphere).

For motor functions, the left hemisphere runs the right side and the right hemisphere runs the left. The only things not contralateral are smell and taste. Your left nostril and the left side of your tongue go to the left hemisphere; right taste elements go to the right.

To locate sounds, we use both hemispheres together, doing the same task. But it is far more common for the hemispheres to provide complementary elements for complex tasks.

The left hemisphere usually handles language vocabulary, while the right handles emphasis and intonation. When drawing an object, we use the left hemisphere for the details and the right one for the overall outline. We use the left hemisphere to identify face-like designs (seeing faces in clouds, in French fries, etc.). We use the right hemisphere to determine if what we see are actual faces.

38. What Do the Hemispheres Do?

The short answer is that they work together. Your brain is like two supercomputers that are networked together. They have some unique qualities but work best together.

Dominant doesn't mean exclusive; it means primary or taking the lead. The hemispheres are most independent when controlling movement. The left hemisphere runs the right side. If you close your right eye or wiggle your right leg, the left hemisphere is doing it. If you move your left arm or clench your left hand, the right hemisphere is running the show.

But when you are using both hands together, both hemispheres (and other parts of the brain system) are working together. Remember trying to pat your head and rub your tummy at the same time? It is hard to do because the two hemispheres haven't practiced together enough. They are like a band who knows their own parts but don't play well together.

The hemispheres are much more practiced in non-motor activities. The left hemisphere is primarily responsible for language, particularly grammar and word production. It is your storytelling hemisphere. But the right hemisphere processes intonation, emphasis, and phrasing.

The right hemisphere is great at pattern recognition. When presented with words like finger, cry, and door, the right will choose a word like pain or smash. When these words are presented to the left hemisphere, the left hemisphere will tell you a whole story about a little boy who had his hands still in the door when his Mom slammed it shut. The left loves to explain how what is happening is related to what has happened in the past and what will happen in the future. The left tells the story, the right extracts the moral. The left hemisphere connects details. The right lives in the moment. The left gives you an encyclopedia. The right gives you a sense of self.

When you draw a figure, the right hemisphere forms the outline and the left hemisphere fills in the details. The right hemisphere looks at the whole. It thinks about spatial relationships. The left processes things sequentially, and thinks about what to do next. The right processes visual imagery; the left insists on logic. The right hemisphere processes music, the left provides the lyrics. The left hemisphere identifies if a cloud looks like a face. The right hemisphere decides if it is an actual face.

39. How Are the Hemispheres Connected?

The hemispheres sit next to each other but are independent of each other. They are completely separate but they sit on a bundle of nerve fibers that functionally connect them: the corpus callosum.

The corpus callosum is a wide, flat bundle of neural fibers under the cerebral cortex which interconnects the two hemispheres. It is not the only connection, but it is the largest. With approximately 250 million myelinated axons, the corpus callosum is the largest white matter structure in the body.

The corpus callosum looks like a modern backless bench or a horizontal letter C. It is flat in the middle and bends under at each end. The forward bend is called the genu (or knee). It contains thin axons, and connects the prefrontal cortexes of each hemisphere. This portion tends to be bigger in musicians.

The flat region is called the truncus, which connects the motor cortexes. These thick neurons connect M1, the premotor and the supplemental motor cortexes. The bend in back is the splenium, which transfers somatosensory information between the parietal and occipital lobes.

The corpus callosum grows slowly, reaching maturity at about 10 years old. In young children, it is easy to see the lack of hemispheric coordination. If you give children two pieces of fabric and ask them which is smoother, three-year-olds will do best if they use one hand. If they hold a piece in each hand, they will have 90% more errors. Five-year-olds do equally well with one or two hands. You can achieve similar results if you try to rub your tummy and pat your head at the same time.

The corpus callosum is the same size in men and women, but it is larger (about 10%) in left-handed folk. No, to anticipate your question, no one knows why. The guess is that the hemispheres must interact more often when hand control is not located where it usually is.

40. What Is A Split-Brain Person?

The corpus callosum is the main connection between the two cerebral hemispheres. When it is cut, the two hemispheres operate more independently, resulting in a split-brain patient. The fibers can be damaged by trauma or severed to as a treatment for severe epileptic seizures. The number of fibers cut or damaged determines the number of symptoms. Some epileptic patients can be helped with only a few fibers connections ablated. Others require more extensive severing.

Once the corpus callosum is severed, the hemispheres operate more independently. You then have no difficulty drawing a different object with each hand: a circle with one, a square with the other. There is no competition between the hemispheres for procedural dominance (taking the lead on any given task). They do their own thing. Right after the surgery, one patient found himself pulling up his pants with one hand while the other hand was trying to pull them down. Another patient angrily grabbed his wife with his left hand until the right hand pulled his left hand away.

But it can get better over time. These odd symptoms are rare and typically last only a few weeks. Most patients are able to adapt to it. Soon it feels normal. They achieve normalcy in a different way. They have no difficulty managing their everyday lives but in a lab you would see they process information much differently.

In a research lab, a subject focuses on a fixation point, like a triangle in the middle of a computer screen. Words or pictures flashed to the right side of the screen are processed in the left hemisphere, where they are easily identified. The left hemisphere, for most people, houses language and encyclopedic information. Finding the correct name for a word or picture is easy.

Flashing a word or picture flashes onto the left side of the screen (goes to the right hemisphere), and subjects often report they "didn't see anything." But when asked to close their eyes and try drawing something with their left hand, they draw a picture of what they actually saw. They saw it but they can't say it because (language isn't in the right hemisphere).

Subjects make the connections outside the brain. They look at what has been drawn. When they open both eyes and look at what they've drawn, the left hemisphere is able to make the connection, and the person says the name of the object. "Oh, it's a cat." It is a discovery that the corpus callosum would have handled internally but now must occur externally.

41. What Is the Temporoparietal Junction?

The answer to "Who am I talking to when I'm weighing options?" might be the temporoparietal junction. This is the spot where the temporal lobe and the parietal lobe come together. It is where the bottom of the parietal lobe sits on the top of the temporal lobe.

This temporoparietal junction gets information from the thalamus, limbic system, parietal lobe and temporal lobe, and integrates it all together. It is basically a processing center for collecting and checking perceptual information.

The parietal lobe processes touch, pain, temperature and spatial relationships. It gives you a 3D view of the world and where you are in it. This information is integrated in the temporoparietal junction with the information from the temporal lobe, which includes memory, language, and auditory and visual data.

The temporoparietal junction (TPJ) uses this combined input to make timing judgments (which sound occurred before the other), remembering names of people and things, identifying lies, and processing social interactions. As this region and the prefrontal cortex develop, children develop a theory of mind. They are able to tell the difference between their thoughts and those of other people. They are able to tell right from wrong and make moral decisions.

The right TPJ seems to pay attention to both externally-generated and self-generated stimuli. It is particularly concerned with activities that occur on your left side and left field of vision. Damage here can reduce awareness of your left arms and legs. It also disrupts spatial recognition of things in the left visual field. The left TPJ pays attention to language, comprehension and understanding the intentions and actions of others. Together they detect when people are lying, process social interactions and influence personal empathy. Damage can impact moral decisions, out of body experiences and the ability to judge the awkwardness of social situations.

42. What Is the Anterior Cingulate Cortex?

The anterior cingulate cortex forms a collar around the corpus callosum. It regulates heart rate and blood pressure, provides error detection, and regulates pain perception. It appears to be involved in decision making, emotional control, and both bottom-up and top-down perceptual processing.

The anterior cingulate cortex has unique neurons called spindle cells. As the name suggests, these neurons are shaped like a spindle. The soma is large but tapers into a single axon. Little is known about their function.

43. Are Mirror Neurons Shiny?

Yes. Mirror neurons are shiny little neurons. They are so shiny you can see yourself. It's like looking in a mirror.

Just kidding.

Mirror neurons are in the supplemental motor cortex of the brain and related regions. This area is just in front of the motor cortex and just behind the prefrontal cortex. How it functions isn't clear. It appears to be involved in coordinating both sides of the body in audition and movement sequences. It may be the stabilization system for walking upright. But also involved in our ability to learn observationally.

Mirror neurons fire when you do something. They also fire when you watch someone else do the same thing. They don't appear to be specially constructed neurons; just a specialized circuit that allows us to learn from watching others.

This ability to mirror the behavior of others is useful in learning and social interaction. We don't have to experience things directly. We can watch others run out of the cave, turn right and get eaten by a sabre tooth tiger. Using this information, we can run out of the cave and turn left.

Mirroring is also helpful in empathy. We feel sad for ourselves when something happens to us. When something happens to someone else, we are able to feel the emotion we would likely feel in similar circumstances. This aids in social interaction. One hypothesis is that people with difficulty relating to others, such as in autism and similar disorders, have problems with their mirror neurons.

44. Why Is There A Seahorse in My Head?

Where else would you put one?

Actually, you have two. One in each hemisphere. Although they are not actual seahorses, each hippocampus looks a bit like a horse or monster. In mythology, a hippocampus is depicted as a horse with the body of a fish. In real life, each looks curved, like the letter C or perhaps the letter S with a small base. They lean inward toward each other and pass through portions of the temporal and frontal lobe.

The hippocampus has connections to both the parietal lobe (location information) and amygdala (emotions). It uses these inputs to make emotional and location-sensitive memories easier to recall. When you go to your childhood home and are flooded with memories of the past, thank your hippocampus for tagging those memories during encoding. Similarly, it is the hippocampus that makes emotional memories easier to find.

The hippocampus is needed to convert knowledge to long-term memory but doesn't seem to be required to recall it. Damage to one hippocampus causes retrograde amnesia, the inability to recall what happened just before the accident. It is like dropping a hard drive while it is still spinning. There is a high likelihood that some data will be lost. Damage to both hippocampi causes anterograde amnesia, the inability to learn new things. It is what stops you from remembering what happened between the crash and waking up in the hospital. Apparently, we need both working together to make sure temporary memories are stored safely away.

45. Where Is the Math Center of The Brain?

There is no one area in the brain dedicated to mathematics. There are several, each serving a different function. The interior temporal gyrus helps us recognize numbers, as opposed to words or nonsense symbols. But if you are looking at a beautiful equation (you get to decide what beauty is), your orbitofrontal region and amygdala are activated.

Mathematics is a complex process and uses many parts of the brain. Actual calculation of numbers occurs in a different place than estimating which number is closer to a target. Einstein said he used mental images more than words, so there are language, visual and spatial factors involved too.

One problem is that we classify things as math that aren't. Learning your multiplication tables is not math. It is learning a list of items. It uses the same processes as learning a shopping list or memorizing state capitals. Memorizing uses semantic memory, which is associated with the medial temporal lobe. Story problems and arithmetic are processed as language, which is associated with the superior temporal lobe.

How numbers relate to each other is spatial memory, associated with the parietal lobe, particularly the intraparietal sulcus. This region is activated when making larger than or smaller than comparisons. Ratios are more about spatial patterns than numbers.

All of these cortical regions working together allows us to create patterns and chunks of information. But even with all of the conscious aspects of mathematics, learning to think in math becomes an automated activity. This means that procedural (implicit) memory is needed for math too. We learn math with our cerebral cortex but soon automate it with our limbic system.

Learning math is like learning a language. We practice the subparts to improve our fluency (easy retrieval of the information when needed). We practice our verb forms and our equation transformations so we can use them when needed. In both language and math, if we don't practice repeatedly how to apply it, both the understanding and the practical applications disappear. Both are use-it-or-lose-it activities.

46. What Is A Primitive Streak?

About the 14th day after fertilization, a dark narrow line begins to show along the dorsal curve of the embryo. Called the primitive streak, it looks like a pen mark on the back of the embryo. This streak will soon flatten out into a plate, the middle will fall down, and the edges will roll up. Cells from each side will connect with each other and pull the edges together forming a neural tube. The closing of the neural tube looks like someone zipped it up.

Created by a complicated network of signaling pathways, the development from a neural streak to a neural tube is an example of bilateral symmetry. Founder cells mirror each other during development. The bottom of the neural tube will become the spine. The upper portion will develop into three bulges: the forebrain, midbrain, and hindbrain.

47. What Are the Forebrain, Midbrain & Hindbrain?

Forebrain. The forebrain is the most anterior of the three bulges (vesicles) that develop out of the neural tube. It is also called the prosencephalon. The forebrain will develop into the cerebrum, thalamus, hypothalamus and most of the limbic system. It includes the brain (cerebrum) and virtually everything under it. All types of memory, sensory detection, and cognitive function will grow out of this region.

Midbrain. The midbrain is between the forebrain and hindbrain in location and in function. How it functions will be easier to understand if we look at the hindbrain first.

Hindbrain. The hindbrain, also called the rhombencephalon, includes the medulla, cerebellum, and pons. These are the structures that sit on top of the spine.

Midbrain (reprise). The midbrain is the connector between the forebrain and hindbrain. Developing out of the neural tube, the midbrain, also called the mesencephalon, is the middle bulge. It will develop into the top of the brain stem, and includes everything from the tectum of top to the tegmentum on the bottom. Nuclei include the superior colliculi (vision), inferior colliculi (audition), the red nuclei (motor coordination), tegmentum (reflexive responses) and the substantia nigra (motor planning).

48. Are the Brains of Men and Women Different?

Mostly no. Certainly not in function. Structurally, men (as a group) have more brain volume but women have thicker cortices. Women have more connections between the hemispheres (20-25% larger corpus callosum and 10-15% larger anterior cingulate cortex). Men have more front to back connections.

In the subcortical areas, there is a similar pattern, maybe. Some studies report men have higher volume in the hippocampus, amygdala, striatum, and thalamus, and women have significantly thicker cortices. Other studies find no difference. The only major subcortical difference is the hypothalamus. A woman's hypothalamus triggers monthly hormonal changes. A man's hypothalamus is not so clever.

Functionally, there is no real difference. No difference in IQ, musical ability, language expression or mathematical functions. All in all, most studies don't need to report data for males and females; there is nothing there.

The brains are comparable but the disorders are not. Although men and women are equally likely to get schizophrenia or bipolar disorder, it is not an even playing field for other problems. Males are 5x more likely to have autism, more likely to die in accidents, more likely to have head trauma and develop Parkinson's disease. Females are twice as likely to acquire depression. They are also more likely to have eating disorders, multiple sclerosis, and thyroid problems. Although men get more strokes and heart attacks, women are more likely to die from them.

49. How Does Light Become Vision?

Light comes at us in waves. Like ocean waves, they vary in height (amplitude) and speed (frequency). The taller the waves, the brighter the light. Amplitude is measured in lumens and lux. Lumens is the amount of energy being emitted in all directions. Lux is the amount of light hitting a specific spot. The sun's lumens remain the same in all directions but its lux on Earth varies from ~20,000 at noon to 400 at sunset to 0 at night.

The speed of waves is measured in the length from peak to peak. Slow waves will have long wavelengths. In contrast, fast waves (high frequency) will have short wavelengths. Short wavelengths are more blue, long wavelengths are more red. Just remember when you see fast blue lights (strobing police car lights), you should put on your slow red lights (your car's stop lights).

The eye focuses the light so it will hit a single spot. The cornea provides most of the focus, but it is fixed and not adjustable. The lens does the other third, and is adjustable. The beam is aimed at the fovea. Receptors on the fovea (cones) react to the light, and release a neural impulse. These impulses leave the eye using the optic nerve. They divide at the optic chiasm so that each hemisphere receives a complete two-eye view of one side of the scene.

The neural pathway stops at the LGN (in the thalamus) but ultimately is processed in the occipital lobe. After processing, two streams of information are passed on to the rest of the brain. The dorsal stream goes from the occipital lobe to the parietal lobe, giving us information about where the object is located. The ventral stream goes from the occipital lobe to the temporal lobe, giving us information about what the object is.

50. How Hard Is It to Fool the Eye?

Not very.

We accept movies as being life-like and they only have 24 frames per second. We aren't fooled into thinking it is real life, but films feel pretty close. High-def TV, at 60, 90 or 120 fps, look real to us; looking through a window kind of real. In contrast, an mp3 audio file recorded at 128,000 samples per second doesn't sound life-like, but it does sound good enough.

Overall, we are quite easily fooled by what we see and rarely fooled by what we hear. Magicians can fool the eye: we like moving objects, we are easily distracted by a sweep of an arm, and we can be fooled to think video displays are real life. But they would fail miserably if they tried to play tricks with what we hear; our sampling rate is much higher, we can detect sounds that are quite faint, and we are not as easily distracted by other sounds.

51. What Is Target Detection?

We have two visual systems. The scotopic system is composed of visual receptors called rods, which respond to light as shades of black and white. This system is extremely sensitive to movement because the rods are located on the peripheral edges of the eye, not the center. It works well in low light situations, and is great for detecting targets but not very good for target identification (the images are too grainy).

The photopic system is 10,000 times less sensitive to light but creates sharp images that are in full color. This system uses cones (instead of rods), works best in bright light, and is great for target identification.

52. How Does Color Vision Work?

The perception of color is a combination of the environment, color receptors, ganglion neurons and the brain. They all work together to provide a full visual experience.

In the environment, light hits an object and reflects off of it. What we see is a combination of distance (between us, the object and the light source), angle (how the light hits), absorption and shine. White objects don't absorb energy, so the entire beam of light is reflected off of it. Black objects absorb all energy, and reflect nothing back. Red objects absorb everything but red. The color which enters our eye is whatever hasn't been absorbed by an object.

In the retina, cones do the initial reaction to wavelengths. The original thought was that there would be three types of cones, one each for red, green and blue. This trichromatic theory proved to be partially true. There are three types of cones, and their ranges overlap, but they mostly vary in how easily they respond to a range of wavelengths. L (long) cones respond to 500-700 nm wavelengths. M (medium) cones respond to 450-630 nms., and the S (short) cones react to 400-500 nms.

After the retina, the ganglia neurons do some additional processing as they carry the signals from the eye to the occipital lobe. These cells compare the response from many different cones, and output three types of information: red-green, blue-yellow and brightness. This opponent-process system helps explain color blindness, which is usually red-green but is never red-blue.

The three types of cones and the three sources of ganglion information are fully processed in the occipital lobe. First, in V1, a low-level description is prepared. Specialized color cells called blobs (an actual technical term) compute cone ratios and compare adjacent scenes. The color cells in V2 form thin stripes that process motion and high-resolution images. They pass on their work to V4, where orientation-selective cells called globs (I kid you not) process more color and form. The output (called the ventral stream) is sent to the inferior temporal lobe for object and face recognition. V1 and V2 outputs also go to V3, which sits directly in front of V2.

Little is known about how V3 functions but it appears to be involved in detecting global motion. It outputs to V5 (also called MT) and then on to the parietal lobe. Somehow the occipital lobe provides color constancy. Although a red shirt outdoors is a different red than when the same shirt is indoors, we see them as the same shade. The brain is providing post-vision processing to overcome the shortcoming of our visual system.

53. Do I Really Have Streams in My Head?

Absolutely; sort of.

Although the body has many fluids, the term stream is usually reserved for a continuous feed of visual information or processing connection. The occipital lobe continuously outputs to both the parietal and temporal lobes. These connections are called streams, in the same way you would stream video online.

54. What Is the Where Pathway?

The dorsal stream, or "where pathway," goes from the occipital
lobe to the parietal lobe. Just remember that if you had a dorsal fin,
it would be on your back, so the dorsal stream runs up the back of
your head. The dorsal stream provides information on which
objects are around you, how they relate to each other and where
you are in this 3D space.

55. What Is the What Pathway?

The ventral stream, or "what pathway," goes from the occipital lobe to the bottom of the temporal lobe. The signals go toward the temples (sides) of your head). The ventral stream provides information about what you are looking at. It allows you to identify objects and faces by looking them up in your mental encyclopedia.

56. How Do We Recognize Faces?

Much of visual processing is done in the occipital lobe but we have specialized regions in the temporal lobes that do the heavy lifting of face identification. After the occipital lobe does the first levels of analysis, it outputs two streams of data. One stream goes to the parietal lobe to figure out where this object is in relations to us and to other objects around us. The other stream goes to the inferior portion of the temporal lobes.

This region in the temporal lobes (called the fusiform gyrus) is where we process faces. Note that we only process upright faces here. That's our specialty. If faces are sideways or upside down, we process them as normal visual data. But if they appear to be an upright face, we use our specialized face-processing system.

Face identification requires we answer three questions: (a) Is this face-like? (b) Is this an actual face? and (c) Whose face is this?

The first step, face detection, is a top-down process built into our visual system. We are constantly looking for things that look like faces. If something might be a face, we send the information to the fusiform gyrus located in the left hemisphere of the brain.

The second step is to confirm that what we are viewing is face-like. The left hemisphere is very good at telling stories. It allows us to look at clouds, and see ships, animals, and faces. When a cut tomato or a piece of potato looks like a face, the left fusiform gyrus verifies that this is indeed true.

The third step is to confirm that we are viewing an actual face. This processing is done by the right fusiform gyrus, and occurs somewhat simultaneously. Both fusiform gyri process face information together and somewhat independently.

There is a fourth step. Convinced that we are looking at an actual face, we look up the "who is that?" information in our normal mental encyclopedia. This process is slower, and not always successful. We are virtually flawless in identifying face-like and actual-face components. But remembering that we went to school with them in second grade can take some time.

On the whole, however, we are much better at remembering faces than we are at matching names to them. We quickly detect and confirm faces. And we quickly categorize them as friend or foe, using the amygdalae. But we don't have specialized processors for categorizing faces as "people I know." Remembering who a person is and how you know them requires a regular personal database search. It is the same as looking up any other fact.

57. What Does the Posterior Parietal Do?

The occipital sends streams of information to the inferior temporal lobe and to the posterior parietal lobe. The temporal lobe identifies objects and faces. The parietal lobe locates objects in relation to us and to each other. It is also involved in mathematics, eye movements, calculations, sensing pain, switching attention, visual working memory, reaching, grasping and spatial reasoning.

The posterior parietal lobe's main job is to tell you where you are and what is around you. It is your internal GPS and mental RADAR. The GPS function centers on you and where you are. The RADAR-like function identifies targets and obstacles around you. Every time you shift your gaze, the posterior parietal lobe remaps itself. Together, this region provides a 3-D view of the world, as it relates to you.

The posterior parietal lobe is quite complex. Some parts of this region are active only when activity is taking place (e.g., moving your arm). Other parts are active during the planning and doing phases. In addition, some regions specialize in arm movement, and others in eye movements. They facilitate your ability to reach, grasp and carry an object. The whole goal of the parietal lobe is to help you interact with the world around you.

When you are learning a skill, which involves moving your hands and arms, the posterior parietal lobe is involved. If you are tracing a maze with your hand or brushing strokes on a painting, this region, particularly the right parietal lobe, is active. The fewer errors you make, the less active it needs to be.

58. How Does the Brain Sense Touch?

When mechanical sensors are pushed down, they activate a neural impulse which travels up the back of the spine, eventually reaching the parietal lobe. This combination of receptors and cortical processing give us the sense of touch.

There are four basic type of touch receptors. Two respond to light touch, two to deep touch. Two provide on-off signals, two continuously fire for as long as they are being pressed.

Think of it as a fourplex apartment or a classic English two-up two-down house. Upstairs, close to the surface of the skin, the Meissner's and Merkl's live. The Meissner's corpuscles (sometimes called tactile corpuscles) have unmyelinated nerve endings that respond to light touch and slow vibrations. They produce on-off signals when there are changes in texture. Meissner's are located in the lips, fingertips, palms of the hands and the foreskin of the penis. You read Braille with the Meissner's.

Next door to the Meissner's, the Merkel's discs are slow-adapting cells that are close to the surface of the skin. They are located in the fingertips and scalp. They provide extremely detailed information about shapes and edges because their receptive fields are small. As long as something is touching your hair, your Merkel's continuously fire.

The Meissner's indicate you touched a coin. The Merkel's report you are still touching the coin. When you stop touching the coin, the Meissner's will fire once, and the Merkel's will stop firing.

Downstairs, deeper in the skin, there are receptors to report on deep touch. The Pacinian corpuscles (also called lamellar corpuscles) provide on-off signals for deep touch and sudden changes (coin leaves the hand). They are unmyelinated, fast adapting (so you can forget you are wearing clothes) and are common in joints (to indicate body position). The Pacinians are the only touch receptor which doesn't also report pain. They only do touch.

The Reffini's end organs (bulbous corpuscles) are deep in the skin, slow adapting (slow reacting), and continuous firing. They report sustained pressure and skin stretch. Like the Merkel's, the Ruffini's indicate where the coin is. Both are also myelinated.

Signals from the touch receptors are sent to the somatosensory cortex in the anterior parietal lobe. This region integrates touch information with other inputs and provides us with our body perception. When the somatosensory cortex is damaged (e.g., Alzheimer's) the result is poor body perception, and difficulty putting on your clothes.

59. How Does the Brain Sense Temperature?

The brain uses itself, the skin, the eyes and the internal organs to measure temperature. There are receptors in the skin, bladder and cornea for measuring external temperature. Internal core temperature is accessed in the preoptic and hypothalamic regions of the brain. The brain then compares the two.

Receptors in the skin send signals up the spinal cord to the thalamus. These temperature reactive receptors form two independent systems. One measures warm, the other measures cold. There is no system for hot. Hot is coded as extreme, making it difficult to tell if it is extremely hot or extremely cold. This paradoxical cold means there is a little delay in moving your hand off a hot stove or a frozen pipe; the brain is trying to figure out which extreme it is.

The receptors are touch receptors. There are no specialized temperature receptors in the skin. All of the touch receptors, except the Pacinian's, report touch, pain and temperature. The free endings of touch neurons don't have to be depressed or mechanically triggered. They simply respond to outside temperatures, compared to the current skin temperature. We are not absolutists in our measurement of temperature. We use physiological zero, where your skin temperature is considered normal, and the new stimulus is judged to be warmer or colder than our skin.

The signals are sent to the brain separately for warm and cold sensations. Warm information is transmitted on thin, unmyelinated C-fibers. These signals are very slow. Cold sensations are transmitted both on C-fibers and A-delta fibers (thin, myelinated). Warm is coded by increasing the firing rate of the neurons. Cooling is coded by decreasing the firing rate of the warm neurons. Cold is coded by decreasing the warm firing rate and increasing the cool firing rate. Some cold receptors also produce a brief pulse at high temperatures.

60. How Does the Brain Detect Body Position?

Vestibular sensations track the position and movement of the head. They measure pressure, bending, neck stretching, spatial orientation and balance. Signals come from the semicircular canals, the otolith organs, and the neck. This information is used to keep you upright, and to control your eye movements.

The muscles in the neck have sensors which detect how much you are stretching them. This helps indicate the vertical location of the head and its angle. Head position is key in your body's ability to maintain balance (keeping body mass of its base and center of gravity).

The otolith organs in the inner ear indicate linear acceleration. They track how fast you are going. There are two otolith organs on each side of the body. The utricle, the larger of the two, detects linear acceleration and degrees of head tilt. The utricle's macula (dip) contains hair cells (cilia) and a weighted membrane embedded with granules (stone-like protein crystals called otoliths). When the head shifts, gravity pulls on the cilia and tilts them in one direction or another. Outputs from the utricle help direct eye movements. By comparing what you see, how much the neck is stretched and how much acceleration the utricles report, the brain can tell if the head is tilted or the whole body.

The saccules operate in a similar fashion as the utricles, but their output is less about eye movement and more about posture. It is smaller and more globular than the utricle. It is also more sensitive to vertical acceleration. When your plane is rushing down the runway for takeoff, the utricles are more activated. When you take an elevator to the top of a high rise, the saccules are more activated.

With two utricles and two saccules to provide information, every position of the head can be tracked. They work independently, providing a whole system which relies on the push-pull of backward-forward acceleration and side-to-side movement. They both provide sensory information about where your body is in space.

The semicircular canals provide information about rotational movements. The canals are fluid filled and work on the same push-pull principle as the otoliths. Each semicircular canal specializes in detecting movement in one direction. They are orthogonal to each (on independent places), so the whole 3-D space is mapped by them. The lateral semicircular canals detect horizontal rotation (pirouettes). The superior semicircular canals track anterior-posterior rotations (head over heels). The inferior semicircular canals report on side-to-side rotation (cartwheels).

The three pairs of semicircular canals work together. They output to the cerebellum, the thalamus, the spine and the eyes. The cerebellum is involved in coordinating movements. The thalamus is the brain's primary switching station, so everything goes through it. The eyes help confirm our movements. The spinal cord produces reflex actions in the trunk and limbs that help us maintain balance.

Damage to the vestibular system results in dizziness, vertigo, nausea, vomiting, and difficulty walking. Most disruptions are temporary, caused by colds, flu, chemicals and head trauma. But some chronic conditions (cervical spine injuries, migraines, epilepsy, Parkinson's and multiple sclerosis) can cause symptoms which never go away.

61. How Do We Perceive Pain?

As a stimulus, pain is attention-getting, unpleasant and surprisingly slow. Attention is required to perceive pain. The brain has to consciously perceive it. Sometimes you can distract yourself to lower the amount of pain experienced. This is the idea behind breathing routines during childbirth or meditation training for chronic pain. Sometimes you want and anticipate pain. If you're about to eat hot chilies or get a massage, pain is part of the pleasure. Both pain and pleasure are sorted out in the brain. It is how you think about them.

It, of course, doesn't work to turn your back pain into pleasure. Pain is unpleasant and distressing. It is trying to get you to slow down or it is reporting that something has broken. Aside from a few pain-pleasure mixtures, pain is no fun.

Pain is slow. It is slow to adapt and slow to reach the brain. Smell adapts extremely quickly. Pain lingers on, depending on which kind it is. The smallest myelinated neurons (A-deltas) carry touch and heat information. They also report sharp pain, telling you to put down the hot frying pan. This sort of pain is good because after you do something (put down the pan) the pain goes away.

C fibers are unmyelinated neurons which carry heat and itch information. They also report dull pain. This sort of pain is bad because it continues after the causal stimulus has been removed. This chronic pain is difficult to treat. Sharp and dull pain are separate systems, and treatments for one are not usually effective for the other.

Mostly pain is detected by bipolar neurons located in the spinal cord. One arm reaches out to a receptor; the other arm sends signals to the brain. They report damage to skin, muscles, joints and internal organs. How much pain is experienced depends on the sensitivity of the receptors, the level of stimulation, and what the brain is currently doing.

We sense pain through four general inputs. First, our thermal receptors report extreme temperatures as pain.

Second, our touch (mechanical) receptors report intense pressure as pain. Note that the Pacinian corpuses report touch only. They don't send pain signals.

Third, inflammation is reported as pain by chemicals released at the same time (what some call silent nociceptors). Inflammation makes the thermal and mechanical receptors more sensitive to pain. Fourth, some receptors respond to everything. These polymodal nociceptors are triggered by temperature, touch, and chemical stressors.

62. How Do We Perceive Itch?

Itch releases histamine. It is released when you damage your skin or come in contact with certain plants. In the brain and spinal cord, it acts as a neurotransmitter (a monoamine). In the peripheral, histamine helps regulate the gut, and aids in repairing wounds (makes it easier for white blood cells to enter the bloodstream). When you have a stuffy nose, you take an antihistamine to block histamine's action. You don't want more blood coming to the aid of your hay fever, you want less. So, you temporarily shut down your immune system's response to the invading pollen hordes.

Itch is slower than other tactile senses. The signals travel only on unmyelinated C fibers. They only go about 2 miles per hour (signals to activate muscles travel at 265 mph). Although itch and some pain sensations use the same type of fibers, and both go to the parietal lobe for processing, but the two systems are independent, and often negatively correlated. As pain goes up, itch goes down. As pain goes down, itch goes up. Opioids decrease pain but increase itch.

Sensitivity to itch is pretty evenly distributed across the skin. Itch acts as an alert to remove whatever is irritating the skin (poison ivy, insects, sunburns, scars, and dandruff). It also occurs as a response to infections (herpes, chickenpox, etc.), changes in hormones (menopause), and medical conditions (eczema, diabetes, iron deficiency, cancer, and schizophrenia).

Itch is typically a peripheral nervous system phenomenon. It reports changes in the top two layers of the skin (not the innermost). There are no itch receptors in the muscles or joints. But itch can be the result of damage to the central nervous system (multiple sclerosis, etc.).

Itching is contagious. Seeing someone else scratch can make up itch. I hate to include itch as a topic because reading about (or writing about it in my case) can causing itching. I think I'll stop.

63. How Does the Brain Sense Sounds?

The usual way we experience sounds involves converting waves of air into neuron impulses. Air hits our outer ear (pinna) in waves. The more frequent the wave, the less distance from the peak of one wave to the next peak (wavelength).

As air waves come toward you, they are collected and funneled into the ear. The pinna (also spelled pinnae) has two jobs.

First, it aids in localization of sound. When you are trying to find where a sound is coming from, you turn your head from side to side, using the pinna as a sound scoop. You might even cup your hand around it to make a larger collector.

Second, the pinna funnels the air waves to the eardrum (tympanic membrane). The tympanic membrane is thin (about 1mm), round (about 9mm in diameter) and cone-shaped like a shield. It is smooth on the pinna side and concave on the middle-ear side. The concave center of the shield (called the umbo) encloses the end of the malleus bone. The tympanic membrane is like a shield on an arm or a knob on a stick. It separates the outer and middle ear spaces. Both spaces are air-filled, and pressure is balanced by the Eustachian tube.

The bones in the middle ear (malleus, incus, and stapes) act as a preamplifier. Vibrations on the tympanic membrane are 20x larger when the stapes strikes the oval window. The oval window separates the middle ear from the inner ear. Vibrations on the oval window push the fluid in the inner ear. The fluid displaces hair-like fibers (stereocilia), which act like pressure sensors and trigger neural impulses.

The neural impulses from the cochlea are sent to the superior region of the temporal lobe for processing of language and music.

Hearing is the transduction of vibrations into neural impulses. Usually, these are outside vibrations from air hitting the ear. But sometimes we can hear inside vibrations. The thalamus produces a synchronizing pulse which sweeps from the front of the brain to the back of it about 40 times a second. These gamma waves from inside the head (not to be confused with gamma rays from atomic radiation) can activate the auditory cortex. This is particularly true of schizophrenic patients. They might be sensitive to gamma waves in the 12–30 Hz range, resulting in auditory hallucinations.

64. Where Does the Brain Process Sound?

Although we collect sound waves with the ear, we process the sounds we perceive in the temporal lobe. The primary projection area for sound is in the superior temporal lobe. It is organized into 3 concentric regions.

The center-most region is the primary auditory cortex. It is tonotopically organized (low frequencies at one end, high at the other), and receives input directly from the MGN of the thalamus. The primary auditory cortex identifies pitch, rhythm and loudness.

The secondary auditory cortex is the next ring out. It further processes sound patterns for harmony, melody and complex rhythms.

The tertiary auditory cortex is on the outside edges. It separates composite audio inputs into individual streams, identifies the location of sounds, and integrates the entire musical experience.

Together with the frontal and parietal lobes, the brain experiences the same note played by different instruments in an orchestra as being both cohesive and distinctly different.

When thinking about music or getting a song stuck in your head, the auditory cortex allows us to experience melody, harmony, and rhythm without actually hearing the sounds. Getting a song stuck in your head is equivalent to visualizing an object or imagining a scene. The projection areas are activated to create the experience, even though the receptor systems are not being used.

65. Where Does the Brain Process Language?

Language is processed in several regions of the brain. It is too important to be limited to one place. Language is essentially a symbolic extraction system. Instead of saving detailed images, we convert it all into symbols we can easily store, quickly retrieve and endlessly generate new patterns and interconnections.

Wernicke's area is the primary center for language comprehension. Located where the temporal and parietal lobes meet, this region sits between the auditory and visual cortices, integrating both inputs. It aids in understanding written words and spoken speech. It parses sounds into words (word recognition), animal noises (what does a cow say?) and machine sounds (cars, trucks, airplanes). When you mimic a sound, Wernicke's area is activated.

There is a Wernicke's area in each hemisphere. This region in the dominant hemisphere does primary word associations, while the non-dominant side resolves ambiguous words and subordinate associations.

Damage to Wernicke's area is called receptive or fluent aphasia because it impairs the ability to understand what others say and to generate coherent language. It does not appear to impact syntax. The damage impacts written, signed or spoken language. Everything you say sounds like gibberish to others, and everything they say sounds like gibberish to you.

Broca's area works in concert with Wernicke's area but specializes in the production of language. This region is in the inferior frontal lobe but its precise location, size, and shape vary greatly between people. Broca's area interacts with the prefrontal cortex, the superior temporal lobe, and the motor cortex, larynx, tongue, mouth, etc.

If damaged or pressured by a tumor, you can understand language but not produce it. You can write but not talk. It is not clear if Broca's area is directly responsible for language production or if it coordinates language processing information, such as phonological and semantic fluency. If the deterioration is slow enough, some speech functions can be taken up by adjacent regions.

The arcuate fasciculus is located between Wernicke's and Broca's areas. It is involved in communication by transferring signals between the two regions.

66. How Do We Process Smell?

Our sense of smell starts in the nose but is processed in other parts of the brain, particularly the temporal lobe and orbitofrontal cortex. Smell (olfaction) is the detection of molecules as they float through the air. When an odorant protein binds to a receptor in the nasal cavity, a multistep depolarization system is activated. The progressive depolarization is mediated by a G-protein.

The signals from a single receptor are combined with those from other receptors in the area. They are aggregated by glomeruli (round structures) in the olfactory bulb, which is located between the amygdala and the temporal lobe. The amygdala provides emotional reactions to smells. The temporal lobe identifies the smell (chocolate, oatmeal & raisins) and stores/retrieves smell-stimulated memories (Gramma's cookies).

Each nostril sends signals to only one hemisphere. The left nostril projects to the left hemisphere, and the right nostril goes to the right hemisphere. Unlike other senses, there is no crossover with smell. If you want to check on the status of a smell, use the same nostril. But remember that adaptation is quite rapid. Smells may linger but not our ability to detect them. That's how we can stand to live with ourselves.

Most of the processing for smell occurs after the fact. The neurons in the orbitofrontal region respond to only one or at most a few orders. The exact mechanism is unknown. We smell but we don't know how or why.

People can detect between 10,000 and a trillion separate odors. The larger number is from more recent research but no one knows what the real number is. It is difficult to research smell because it is quite complex. We have about 10 million receptors, plus plenty of tufted cells, mitral cells, periglomerular cells, short axon cells and astrocytes involved. Smell uses several neurotransmitters too, including acetylcholine, serotonin, and norepinephrine.

What makes research so overwhelmingly challenging is that the cells in the nose are replaced every 12-14 days, the nostrils switch primacy every few hours, and the mucous is replaced every 10-12 minutes. It is a very active system.

In fact, it is two active systems. We have a primary and a secondary olfactory system. The primary olfactory system identifies the chemical structure, distinguishes between odors, and categorizes smells as attractive or aversive.

The secondary system is quite limited in humans. How limited is a matter of some controversy. In other animals, this system is used for detecting pheromones. In humans, its pathway appears to be truncated. There is no conscious recognition of whatever the secondary olfactory system can detect. Some believe the limbic system can use this information. The only experimental evidence of pheromone detection in humans is based on the observation that the monthly periods of women who live together (in the same house or dorm) tend to synchronize.

67. What Is Memory?

Memory is a series of systems which generative "memory events" from stored elements. You don't have a bad memory; it is not a single thing. You have multiple memory systems, some of which work better than others.

We limit the amount of data to store by extracting meaning. We don't see a field of flowers and encode "flower, flower, flower, flower…" We say "pretty" and store that statement and emotion.

We store the recipe, not the whole meal. We make notes about an item or event: its location, objects (and people) present, time of day, weather, emotion, spatial information, importance and relationship to other things we know. When we remember, we re-member (put parts together) or re-collect (reconstitute). Every memory is generated new upon demand. They make us adaptable to our environment but prone to alter and reinterpret our memories.

We use the hippocampus to generate simplified patterns from our original information. During the night, we consolidate complex patterns into sparse encodings which are more easily stored in long-term memory. We don't need the hippocampus to pull things out of long-term memory, just to put them in.

In addition to this semantic processing of words and events, we have a separate system for learning and remembering continuous motions (swimming, running and riding a bicycle). This "muscle memory" is not stored in the muscles; it is its own distinctive style of memory.

We have a memory system for upcoming events (procedural memory), sensory inputs (echoic memory and iconic memory), for rules (procedural memory) and for things we are currently thinking about (working memory). We have multiple memory systems, each doing its own thing.

68. Why Do I Have Such A Bad Memory?

You don't.

First, you have a single memory system. Memory is the result of multiple systems. They do separate things but they all work together. When one system fails, the others continue to work.

Second, your memory probably hasn't changed much. As we get older, we blame our memory failures on age. Truth is, most people often can't find the right word. "It's on the tip of my tongue" occurs to most people regardless of age, usually about once a week. When we're young, we don't blame it on anything. We just accept it. When we are old, we assume our memory systems are to blame.

Third, you are probably talking about one of three types of memory. As we get older, we notice that we forget to go to appointments or other events. This is prospective memory. Often these failures come from not checking a calendar or not carrying a daily planner. When we are old, we have the same schedule day to day, so we have fewer cues to remind us to go to meetings or events. With smartphones, problems with prospective memory are greatly reduced.

You might be referring to semantic memory, the kind you use when studying for a class. As we age, we find it harder to learn new things. Mostly this is because we don't remember how hard it was to learn new things when we were young. Learning vocabulary terms is hard, has always been hard and will continue to be hard. Semantic memory is sensitive to the use-it-or-lose-it rule. If you don't study on a regular basis, learning is harder. Think of it like a second language. If you haven't used your high school French for years, you will recall very little of it. You have to use it to remember it. Semantic memory drops off rapidly. Learn a list of words and you'll find that the next day, you've lost a lot of them. Age has little to do with it. Semantic memory actually improves as you age.

Episodic memory, stories about what we've done, fade at a constant rate. Your childhood memories are a bit less clear every year. Partly, this is due to having added more experiences to your storage. The more memories you have to keep track of, the more interference between them. You might try to pull out a memory from 10 years ago and accidentally grab things from 8 years ago. It is like reaching into a cupboard for a pot, grabbing a handle and pulling, only to discover the one you have in hand is not the one you expected. These retrieval errors are a common occurrence.

In general, memory loss is not a function of age. It is a function of practice and lifestyle. When you meet someone, try to store it. Say it out loud to make sure you have the pronunciation correct. Write it down so you have spelling correct. Focus on the getting-it-into-memory process. If you've encoded things properly, you'll find the getting-it-out-of-memory process is relatively easy. Practice remembering. Make it a part of your lifestyle.

69. How Do I Improve My Memory?

The key is to only learn things you want to remember long term. If you don't want to remember it, write it down. Writing things down reduces your cognitive load and frees you to do more important things. If you are going to the store, write down your shopping list. Remembering details is not our best ability. And you don't want to remember milk, banana, potatoes long term. You only want to remember them long enough to buy them. Write down lists like this. Only store in your head things you want to remember for a long time.

If you want to remember things long term, use my BET method.

B is for body. The best thing you can do for your memory is to be physically healthy. For most people, this means to eat reasonably, exercise sufficiently, and sleep longer. There are no magic pills or supplements you need for your memory. You should fill deficiencies but otherwise leave your body alone. The key to a good memory is don't get sick.

E is for encoding. The biggest reason we don't remember something is that we don't put it into memory. We don't remember names when we're introduced to someone because we don't focus on them. We're thinking about us, our nervousness, and what we're going to say next. Start with paying attention.

T is for testing. The only way to know if something is still in memory is to check. Every once in a while, try to retrieve the things you want to remember. If you remember them, you can wait longer before you check again. If you don't remember them, shorten the time for your next retrieval check.

70. How Do I Keep My Childhood Memories from Fading?

Photographs. The best way to remember your childhood is to periodically go through your photo albums and home movies. Reviewing the past will help reinstate details you had forgotten.

Photos are a strong tool for memory. One study asked people to provide a series of photos of them and their family members doing things. The pictures showed a variety of activities but all shared one quality: none of the subjects had ever been in a hot air balloon. The researchers created a fake photo of each subject and one of their family members inside a hot air balloon. After a week of viewing all of their pictures every day, half of the subjects remembered being in a hot air balloon. It only took a week to plant this fake memory.

Instead of planting fake memories, you can use photos to add detail to your existing memories. Take a group of pictures and review them. Go back through your childhood remembering each event and all of the people who were there. You will re-encode these events with memories that have more detail, more familiarity and more staying power.

71. Where Is Memory Stored?

Most of what we know about where memories are stored comes from people who have lost function in portions of their brains. This tells us that a particular region is needed to access those memories but it doesn't tell us if they are stored there. It could be that a region is needed to access memories but that it is in fact stored somewhere else.

We know four things about where memories are stored and we have some guesses about how they are stored.

We know that the dorsolateral portion of the prefrontal cortex (part of the frontal lobe) is required for working memory (un-stored memory). Damage here doesn't affect previously stored information but it prevents us from working on current information.

We know that the hippocampus is required to transfer things to long-term memory but isn't needed for retrieving them. It aids in the consolidation process but is not involved in getting things out of long-term storage.

We know that the temporal lobes are required for semantic and episodic memory. They work together but the left temporal lobe seems to do much of the work for semantic memories (words, facts, etc.). The right temporal lobe seems to take the lead for episodic memories (events).

We know that the limbic system is required for implicit memory (how to drive a car, ride a bike or swim). Anything that is a continuous movement (peddling, spinning, arms strokes) is learned a little at a time in the limbic system.

We are guessing that memories are distributed across the brain. It seems that the brain operates like a giant collection of redundant hard drives. Damage to one area doesn't necessarily destroy memories because there are backup copies in other parts of the brain.

We are guessing that memory is stored in neural circuits, not as an actual physical unit. Historically, researchers looked for engrams: parts of the brain that are physically changed when a memory is present. Instead of a structural unit, most researchers now believe memories are more virtual. They are circuits or patterns of neural firings. But no one knows.

72. Is Déjà Vu Memories from Past Lives?

Sorry, no. Déjà vu is an unexpected emotional reaction to a memory retrieval error. You're trying to pull out a memory but getting an emotional response that doesn't match. In déjà vu (literally again-see or before-see), you search your memory banks and they report you've never been here before. But it does report an emotional cue is present.

When we store a memory, it is tagged with spatial, emotional, temporal and associational cues. We store the fact itself and a tiny bit of information about where we are spatially in relationship to objects and other people. We store an emotional tag, a time stamp and some key words of similar experiences. In déjà vu, our memory search pulls out an emotional tag (probably from another memory or a previous dream) and delivers it to consciousness. We get the emotional cue but no memory is attached.

Déjà vu can be caused by drugs or epilepsy. Mixing drugs to treat the flu can cause déjà vu side effects, probably related to increased activity of dopamine-releasing neurons. Epileptic activity in the temporal lobes often produces déjà vu experiences. The medial region of the temporal lobe is where the hippocampus resides. It is the hippocampus which encodes all of the tags into our long-term memories.

Jamais vu is a related phenomenon in which no emotional cue is present. All the other cues come but not the emotion. You know you've been there before but it doesn't feel familiar. A similar but more extreme condition (Capgras delusion) is caused by damage to the connections between the amygdala and the cerebral cortex. Usually the result of a car crash or other brain trauma, patients report that their home, dog, and family are imposters. They look like the real thing but they aren't. Until the amygdala and cerebral cortex reconnect (usually in a few weeks), the emotional expected reactions aren't present.

There are other experiences where our emotions provide misleading cues. In presque vu, you feel like you're on the edge of a great breakthrough. Something wonderful is about to happen. In déjà rêvé (already dreamed), you feel that the present moment is like a dream you've had before. When we get bits and portions of cues and memories, all kinds of weird experiences occur. When memories and emotional cues are retrieved together, everything feels normal.

73. What Is Declarative Memory?

There are two types of long-term memory: explicit and implicit memory. Explicit memory (declarative memory) is conscious memory. It includes facts, events and all the things you know. You are aware of explicit memory and can declare what you know; you can say it and explain it.

In contrast, implicit memory (procedural memory) is filled with what you can do. You might not be able to explain how you do your jump shot or make things happen on your computer with a keyboard shortcut. You know how to do it but you can't say (declare) how.

Declarative memory requires the hippocampus to form new memories. Implicit memory uses the basal ganglia. Declarative memory keeps track of which dances songs you've learned and whether you went to the prom or not. Implicit memory keeps track of how to actually dance.

Declarative memory has two parts: semantic memory and episodic memory. Semantic memory is your mental encyclopedia of facts. Episodic memory remembers what you did last night and where you were last summer. Semantic memory knows that the capital of Texas is Austin. Episodic memory tells you whether you've ever been to Austin or not.

Semantic and episodic memory systems work together. Semantic memories are like islands of facts. Episodic memories provide a mental map which links those islands together. Semantic memory hosts facts, concepts, and our general knowledge of the world. Episodic memory hosts our personal experiences with the world. Together they optimize your ability to retrieve information.

The hippocampus is required to form new declarative memories, both semantic and episodic. When the hippocampus matures, at about age three or four, there is a major shift in the ability to form spatial, verbal and episodic memories. These are also among the initial faculties to deteriorate in Alzheimer's disease, which impacts the hippocampal region first. Young adults primarily use the left hippocampus but older adults use both.

Declarative memory requires and is enhanced by the neurotransmitter epinephrine, which aids in memory consolidation. Blocking epinephrine interferes with the ability to form new semantic and episodic memories. Visual memories are improved by an increase in acetylcholine, and verbal episodic memories respond well to an increase in other catecholamines. Drugs such as amphetamines increase all of these neurotransmitters, resulting in better general memory formation and in memories which are related to drug administration. For people have been addicted to drugs, epinephrine makes it more difficult to forget where and who they took drugs with, and makes it more likely that these environmental cues can act as relapse triggers.

Cortisol, our primary stress hormone, also impacts the hippocampus. Although cortisol shuts down digestion and immune system responses, at low to medium doses it increases attention, blood flow, and memory consolidation. If we survive the saber tooth tiger, we want to be able to remember it. But high levels of cortisol inhibit episodic memory recall. We might be storing the scary things that are happening now but we're not comparing it to previous experiences. MDNA (ecstasy) works the same way. High doses impair episodic memory retrieval.

74. What Is Semantic Memory

Semantic memory, a type of declarative memory, is part of our meaning-extraction process. It is our personal dictionary and mental encyclopedia. It stores word meanings, facts, concepts, and ideas. All of our general knowledge is stored here. Semantic memory includes semantics (word knowledge), and what we know about objects, language, people in general and the world at large.

Semantic memory tells you what a horse is but not about riding one at summer camp. It tells you that the Golden Gate Bridge is in San Francisco but not if you've ever been there. It tells you what potato chips look like but not about the food fight you had at lunch. Semantic memory handles the "whats" of life.

75. What Is Episodic Memory?

Episodic memory, a type of declarative memory, tracks the who, where and when of your life. It stores our autobiographical stories.

Episodic memory often comes to you in images or little slices of video. It keeps a loosely chronological log of your life. It is particularly interested in you and your interests. In episodic memory, you are the hero of your story. Events may be distorted to make you look good but the bias is consistent and reliable.

The right prefrontal cortex is highly involved in forming new episodic memories. The right hemisphere is often associated with episodic memory (and the left hemisphere for semantic memory) but both sides work together so closely the distinction is probably not helpful.

Episodic memory has strong ties to emotion. When you return to your childhood home, the location cues flood you with episodic memories, complete with emotion, sights, sounds, and smells. Usual events (where you were when a major tragedy occurred) have many cues and form extremely vivid episodic memories called flashbulb memories. They seem to us to be frozen in time, as if captured by a photograph. We tend to repeat the stories and relive them many times. This rehearsal plus the strong emotional cues make these experiences very vivid. They are not more accurate but more likely to be recalled.

Flashbulb memories include your most embarrassing experiences, your greatest achievements, and national and international news events. I clearly remember where I was on Sept 11, 2001, the day my father died, and when we had to break a window to get back into the house (I was three). I also vividly remember my high school graduation, my first day of grad school, and the first time I heard a song I'd written playing live on the radio. Episodic memory is like having a highlights reel of your life. Episodic memory reports what happened, where it happened and when it happened. Semantic memory reports what we previously knew about the topic, our current level of knowledge and speculations about what will happen in the future.

Although our episodic memories are vivid, they are not necessarily accurate. We lose a lot of the details from our original experience. The events feel reliable but they often aren't.

Some animals have episodic-like memories. Hummingbirds can remember how long it has been since they've been somewhere and which flowers are there. But they don't have the semantic capabilities needed to extrapolate beyond current conditions. And they don't have the episodic memory system needed to optimize semantic knowledge.

Semantic and episodic memory systems work together. Semantic memories are like islands of facts. Episodic memories provide a mental map which links those islands together. Semantic memory hosts facts, concepts, and our general knowledge of the world. Episodic memory hosts our personal experiences with the world. Together they optimize your ability to retrieve information.

76. What Is Spatial Memory?

Spatial memory keeps track of where you are in your environment. To accomplish this feat, it combines a representation of the world and a representation of you. It calculates the relative positions of items in the environment and where you are in relation to that space. Several regions of the brain are involved in this complex task.

The parietal lobe remaps itself every time you change your gaze. It recalculates your location and those of known objects. This allows you to navigate around a room, around your house and around your neighborhood.

In short-term memory, spatial memory allows you to remember locations (keys are on the table) and spatial relationships (table is behind the couch, across from the windows and under the painting). Both are helpful in navigating through your environment. In Baddeley's theory of working memory, short-term spatial memory is a subprocess. It is a sort of temporary sketchpad.

We remember spatial information the same way we remember paintings. We use a hierarchy, which pretty well matches the steps you'd take if painting a scene. First, we remember the general, overall layout. Think of it as a page view. Second, we remember landmarks and where they fit in the scene. Third, we remember details. This superordinate-ordinate-subordinate process allows us to quickly make ordinal relationships (this is above that but below the other thing). Using this information, we can create a cognitive map we can reference in order to create a new route when needed.

We generate two types of cognitive maps: bearing and sketch. Bearing maps use vectors. They allow you navigate by going North for 1.2 miles, turn NNE for .3 miles and heading West for 20 feet. Sketch maps allow you to navigate by landmarks. You can drive until you see the big tree, turn left and continue until you cross the wooden bridge, and stop at the third house on the right.

Using these two systems we can create routes which optimize for the shortest distance or for maximizing priorities (driving the kids all over town to get them from school to dance to pizza to chess club). The hippocampus then uses this information to tag our memories for location information. The ventral aspects of the hippocampus seem most involved with spatial memory, while the dorsal regions move things from short-term to long-term memory (consolidation).

77. What Is Working Memory?

Working memory is not the opposite of non-working or failed memory. It is memory which is limited to the items you are currently working on, such as reading this sentence.

The term was coined by George Miller, who is best known for his article "The Magical Number Seven, Plus or Minus Two." Miller maintains that working memory is limited to seven items, or seven chunks of 3-4 items, plus or minus two. Most people can keep seven digits in their head, or seven letters, or seven symbols. Some people are better than others, some content is easier than others, but overall, you can only manage about seven units of information.

The easiest analogy is to think of your computer. If your computer crashes while you are writing a sentence, everything is lost. Files must be stored on disc or in the cloud (somebody else's disc) for them to be saved. Working memory is the RAM memory of your computer. Turn the computer off without saving, all your current work is lost. Think about something different than what you're reading and all is lost; you have to re-read the sentence or paragraph.

As long as we keep our focus on the material at hand, it can stay in working memory for quite a long time. This is probably the function of the ventromedial cortex. It helps maintain items in working memory while we focus on them. Higher level processing, the more "working" part of working memory occurs in the dorsolateral cortex.

It is clear that working memory occurs in the prefrontal cortex, probably. It certainly is true that if the prefrontal cortex is damaged, so it is working memory, but the exact location and method of storage is open to debate. The brain works together as a single unit. Multiple portions of the brain often interact with each other, so limiting all versions of working memory to one location is out of character with how the brain usually works.

Some think working memory is part of long-term memory. It is difficult to know what is short-term and what is long-term memory. Learning a list in order requires remembering items from the beginning, which is more long-term than remembering the most recent items. But how long-term is it?

A more helpful approach is to describe the elements which have to be part of any explanation of working memory. Alan Baddeley's multicomponent model proposes four components to working memory, which could be located in different parts of the brain.

First, there is the phonological loop. We process sounds (particularly language) differently than images. Listening is an essential part of how we process information. Reading is the process of converting visual symbols into sounds. The phonological loop is part of that process. Second, there is a visuospatial sketchpad. It processes visual and spatial information we are currently handling. Third, there is an episodic buffer which acts like a timing chain to sequence the work of the other two units. Fourth, there is a central executive which determines who does what, selects what to attend to, and generally runs the show.

78. What Is A Nervous Breakdown?

Nerves don't actually break. They continue to work fine. Your nerves are not fragile. The nerves don't break but they send reports to the brain that trouble us. We get repeated messages of unspecified impending doom. What the nerves are reporting is that our calm and confidence are breaking down. People do experience overwhelming feelings of stress and anxiety.

The alternate "mental breakdown" isn't any better. Your brain is not a car. It doesn't break down. It continues to send signals, process information and generate thoughts and emotions. The nerves are working fine. They are carrying signals from one region of the brain to another. The problem is that these signals are interpreted as being crushingly stressful. People feel overloaded with stimuli, pressured to make decisions, and emotionally empty or blunted.

Depression and anxiety are the main symptoms of these personal crises. But the list is general and encompasses weight loss, weight gain, insomnia, too much sleep, exhaustion, increased blood pressure, dizziness, trembling, immobility, panic attacks, lack of fear, mood swings, and lack of mood swings.

Feeling like you're having a nervous breakdown can lead you to get help. But think of it as a temporary state. It is more of a generalized panic attack than anything else. You get overwhelmed by stress and don't know what to do. Most cases occur after a divorce, romantic breakup, problems at work, or major financial setbacks.

Physical fatigue and health issues are also primary causes. When your system is rundown, you're overworked and you've lost the love of your life, having a crisis is not unexpected. Just remember that it is not a wiring problem. Your issues are fixable. Your hardware is fine. You just need a software update.

79. What Is Amnesia?

Amnesia is a major loss (usually temporary) of memory. Working memory, implicit memory and sensory buffers still function but declarative and prospective memories are mostly or completely gone. You can read, walk and process incoming information but you don't remember major chunks of time.

Amnesia occurs when the hippocampus is damaged. Mild damage causes a temporary disruption in memory encoding (putting things into memory). If one hippocampus is rattled or hurt, you can't remember what happened just before your opponent knocked you out. This retrograde amnesia occurs because your memories during that period were not properly stored (consolidated).

Damage to both sides of the hippocampal system results in not being able to remember what happened between the knockout punch and when you woke up in the hospital. Severe damage could interfere with your ability to acquire new knowledge.

Major anterograde amnesia makes it impossible to move out of the present moment. There is no way to keep track of what you were talking about or to whom. Without the hippocampi, we are lost in the now of life. You can read a sentence and understand it, but if you look up at the clock, the sentence is gone. You can look at a person and smile. Look away and back again, you have no memory of having previously seen them. It is a brand new experience for you. Everyone around you are going on with their conversations but you keep waking up in the middle of a conversation you know nothing about. It is a shock to you but no one seems surprised that you are suddenly awake and listening.

In addition to consolidating memories, the hippocampi are involved in spatial reasoning and navigation. They work with the medial temporal lobes and posterior parietal lobes to integrate spatial reasoning data for the prefrontal cortexes. Using a complex network of place cells, boundary cells and grid cells, the hippocampus helps you track where you physically are. It also helps create cognitive maps.

80. Do You See Stars If Hit on The Back of The Head?

Yes. Or at least, possibly.

The eyes are in the front of the head, just under the frontal lobe of the brain, but the visual information is processed in the occipital lobe, which is located in the back of the head. Receptors in the occipital lobe are triggered by neurons coming from the eyes. But they can sometimes be triggered by trauma to the back of the head. This mechanical activation doesn't produce precise stimulation of specific receptors. A hit of the head gives a broad, diffused impact on a whole region of the occipital lobe. The result appears as lines or stars. You are seeing without your eyes.

Some science fiction writers have proposed that we will eventually be able to bypass the eyes and input directly into the occipital lobe. That would require a great deal more detailed precision than a bump on the head. There are millions of little neurons processing visual information which would have to be individually hooked up to whatever cyber-sensor our robot overlords create.

81. What Are Brain Tumors?

A tumor is a mass of cells growing where it is not supposed to be. It can cause no problems (benign), cause some problems (benign but putting pressure on the brain) or it can grow rapidly while destroying tissue around it (cancerous). Primary tumors originate in the brain. These are uncommon because the brain is so isolated from the rest of the body. Only 2% of brain cancers start in the brain.

Secondary tumors start somewhere else and travel to the brain through the blood or lymph system. Normally, the blood-brain barrier keeps them out but inflammation and local infections can weaken the BBB, allowing the metastasized cells to enter. The most common source of secondary tumors is lung cancer.

Tumors vary in location and rate of growth. If they are slow growing and somewhere that doesn't cause a problem, tumors are just extra passengers. There is no hurry or need to worry. Tumors are bad when they are in a location that causes the brain to not to work as well. Symptoms vary from headaches to sensory disruptions to brain damage.

Rate of growth is also important. It is a fair indicator of cancer (fast-growing tumors are more likely to be cancerous) and urgency (it will eventually cause trouble even if it isn't cancerous). All in all, try not to get a brain tumor. And remember that you probably won't. They aren't that common.

82. What Are the Most Common Brain Tumors?

Tumors in the meninges lining between the brain and skull are not brain tumors (because they aren't in the brain tissue) but they can cause symptoms by giving the brain less space (squeezing it). This is the most common type of tumor. They grow slowly and often aren't cancerous.

The most common type of brain tumor in children is medulloblastoma. These are usually located in the back and bottom of the skull, near the fourth ventricle and the cerebellum. Although noninvasive, medulloblastoma rapidly spread through the cerebrospinal fluid. They start in one location but grow in new areas (metastasize). The survival rate is typically 50-60%.

As the tumor grows, it puts pressure on the brain. At first, a child will be listless or complain of a headache. As the pressure gets worse, they begin to stumble and fall, followed by impairment of both sensory and motor neurons.

In adults, meningiomas and gliomas are the most common primary brain tumors. Gliomas are tumors that involve glial cells, and include astrocytomas, ependymomasependymonas and oligodendrogliomas.

Oligodendrogliomas develop out of myelinating cells in the brain (oligodendrocytes). To insulate and prevent accidental firing, oligodendrocytes wrap around the neurons in the brain to form a buffer between them. In rare cases, they wrap around capillaries to form a matrix and allow cancers to grow.

Similarly, the epithelial lining of the ventricles can become misshapen and allow tumors to grow. Instead of round and regular, these fibrous cells create a launch pad for tumors. In adults, ependymomas are usually in the spinal cord.

83. What Are Astrocytomas?

Astrocytomas are tumors that develop out of astrocytes, star-shaped glial cells that seem like they are involved in everything. Astrocytes are part of the blood-brain barrier, hold neurons in place, and aid in the reuptake of neurotransmitters. They are plentiful and highly useful. Consequently, astrocytomas are a fairly common type of brain tumor, keeping in mind that brain tumors aren't common at all.

Tumors that grow from astrocytes typically don't metastasize (spread) to other parts of the body. They stay in the brain and spinal cord. Some astrocytomas are noninvasive (pilocytic astrocytoma, pleomorphic xanthoastrocytoma, and some that are called subependymal giant cell astrocytoma) They have narrow zones of infiltration. Other astrocytomas spread out in more diffuse infiltration patterns. These include glioblastoma, and anaplastic astrocytoma). There are a lot of subtypes because there are so many astrocytes, and so many things can go wrong with them.

84. What Are Hemangioblastomas?

Hemangioblastomas are rare tumors that occur most often in the spine or cerebellum but they can occur anywhere you have small blood vessels. Stromal cells are non-malignant connective cells but they can form a structural matrix on which cancer cells can grow. When they occur in the occipital lobe, they cause your vision to be distorted or split it into two separate unintegrated images. When they occur in the cerebellum, your ability to coordinate movements is impacted. Hemangioblastomas mostly develop in middle age, and affect more women than men. Diagnosis is usually by a CT scan. Once surgically removed, prognosis is good. Only about 20% develop additional tumors.

85. Does Brain Surgery Hurt?

No. The process sounds bad, but it hurts about the same as cutting your finger.

There are three steps in brain surgery: cutting the skin, drilling through the skull and cutting the brain tissue. The last two don't hurt. Cutting the skin covering the skull hurts about the same as cutting the skin anywhere else. Neither bones or neurons contain pain receptors, so you experience no pain. It sounds like it should hurt, but brain surgery is pretty much pain free.

86. What Is A Stroke?

Strokes are the heart attacks of the brain. When bloodflow to the heart is cut off, it is a heart attack. When bloodflow to the brain is cut off, it is a stroke. There are two general types of strokes, and one preliminary version.

If the symptoms of a stroke last less than 24 hours, it is called a transient ischemic attack. Sometimes called a mini-stroke, TIAs are a warning that something is wrong with the blood supply to your brain. Either there is a narrowing of the blood vessels or a clot is slowing the flow, or both. Blood vessels narrow because they become less elastic or because of plaque. Plaque is typically a combination of fat, cholesterol and other ingredients that are stuck together.

Clots are gel-like clumps of blood that have dislodged from their origin and float freely through the blood. They can get stuck when they reach a spot that is too narrow for them to pass through. If the clot blocks a blood vessel in the heart, it's a heart attack. If the clot blocks a blood vessel in the brain, it's a stroke or TIA.

A typical TIA only lasts a minute or two. The clot dissolves on its own and flow is restored to the brain. Usually, there is no damage to the brain. But people with TIAs are at higher risk of having major strokes. It is a TIA if the symptoms last less than 24 hours. If you die within that time period, it's a stroke.

87. What Is A Hemorrhagic Stroke?

The least likely strokes are hemorrhagic, meaning there is a leaking of blood into the brain. There are two types of hemorrhagic strokes: aneurysms and AVMs. Aneurysms are ballooning regions of a blood vessel. If it bursts, blood rushes into the brain destroying its cells and no blood reaches the cells downstream of the rupture. Although rare, these are the most likely type of stroke to kill you.

Aneurysms can be congenital but they also can form as a result of age and high blood pressure. As we age, our blood vessels lose some of their strength. Similarly, high blood pressure pushes from the inside of the blood vessels and weakens the capillary walls. Taken together, elderly people with high blood pressure are at a higher risk for strokes.

AVMs are arteriovenous malformations. They are congenital structural problems. In normal development, arteries carry oxygen to the brain, where it is used by the neurons. The veins then carry less oxygenated blood back to the heart. An AVM is a tangle of blood vessels which causes the oxygenated blood from the arteries to go straight into the veins and be carried away from the brain. AVMs occur only in about 1% of the population. Their cause is unknown but doesn't seem to be genetic.

88. What Is an Ischemic Stroke?

You are much more likely to have an ischemic stroke, which probably won't kill you but will leave you disabled. About 85% of strokes are ischemic.

The first type of ischemic stroke is caused when a blood clot (thrombus) forms in your brain and blocks one of the arteries leading to your brain. The result can be reduced blood flow (atherosclerosis), loss of blood flow to specific regions of the brain (disability) or no blood flow to the whole brain (resulting in death). Disability is particularly likely to affect the hands and arms (also the legs and feet).

The second type of ischemic stroke is an embolic stroke. This type of stroke is the result of a clot forming somewhere else in the body (usually the heart), going to your brain and blocking an artery.

89. What Is A Concussion?

A concussion is an injury to the brain. It is the result of hitting your head on something or getting hit in the head by something. Most occur when young people are doing sports, but crashes (car and motorcycle), running into tree limbs, and slipping on tile floors also cause them.

Concussions are closed-head injuries. Everything looks normal from the outside. There is no blood, the skull isn't broken, and no brain tissue is visible. Hits and falls are the most common causes of closed-head injuries.

In open-head injuries, the skull is broken and parts of the brain are exposed. Bullets are the most common causes of open-head injuries.

Both types of brain injury vary in severity from mild (concussions) to moderate to severe (traumatic brain injuries). Although severe damage is more likely in combat (from bombs, mortars and explosions), you can have a TBI from playing football or falling off your motorcycle. The cause isn't important. It's the result.

90. Should You Go to The Hospital for A Concussion?

Yes. If the brain injury is severe, getting help early on is the right thing to do. If the injury is mild, then you don't need to go. But since there is no way to know for sure if a concussion is mild or severe, go.

In general, get to the doctor as soon as possible. Hit the emergency room if the person is unconscious (for more than a few seconds), vomits multiple times, if the headache gets worse, if there are seizures, and if symptoms continue. You want to make sure there is adequate oxygen, blood flow, etc.

In an emergency setting, three things should be done: a neurological exam, a CT scan, and an EEG. The neurological exam includes PERRLA (pupils equal, round, reactive to light and accommodation) and the Glasgow Coma Score (a measure of consciousness).

A CT scan is the way to go for structural issues. You don't want to find empty space. X-rays won't find anything in mild cases and do not provide enough detail in severe cases. You're looking for intracranial pressure, internal bleeding and structural damage. Later on, a functional MRI can provide more detail if needed.

In terms of function, an EEG is a quick and accurate way to identify non-normal brain activity. A baseline EEG prior to the injury is helpful but an EEG in combination with vitals and the neurological exam can provide helpful information.

High intracranial pressure can result in death. There can be weakness on one side of the body, and a blown pupil (not constricting to light). The medical staff will check for Cushing's triad (slow heart rate, high blood pressure, and depressed breathing), an indicator of intracranial pressure. Further investigation may involve inserting a catheter into the ventricle of the brain.

91. Where do Alzheimer's tangles occur?

As we age, it is not uncommon to develop some tangles and a few bits of plaque. The result is a few neurons die off. In Alzheimer's, the quantity and rate of development are both much higher. The result is the loss of massive amounts of brain matter and a complete disruption of life.

Alzheimer's moves through the brain, region by region. By the end, nearly all regions have been impacted and show loss of neurons. The brain dies a bit at a time.

Although the rate of progression varies with the person, Alzheimer's disease does follow a similar path. In general, Alzheimer's moves from the front of the brain to the back. The first region affected is the hippocampus and medial temporal lobes. The next region is the prefrontal cortex, usually the orbitofrontal region and then spreading to the dorsolateral and ventromedial areas. The third region impacted is the top of the temporal lobe, where language is processed. The fourth region is the parietal lobe. The fifth region is the motor cortex and cerebellum. And the last regions are the occipital lobes and brain stem.

These are not set stages, and there need not be a complete loss of function of an area. Some islands of neurons will remain healthy and functional, while the rest of the region dies off. Connections are made, not made, and made again, giving the "good day" or "bad day" variation.

Plaque is outside the cells. Tangles are inside the cells. Plaque is a collection of protein bits that get stuck together. They form between neurons and interrupt the triggering of neighboring neurons. Tangles are caused by a neuron's structural components breaking down. When it loses its support system, a neuron's axon gets tangled up with itself, interrupting its triggering of neighboring neurons. If neurons can't communicate with other neurons, they die. Alzheimer's either causes or is caused by neurons losing their ability to interact with other neurons, resulting in their eventual death.

92. What Are the Main Causes of Blindness?

There are four major causes of acquired blindness: glaucoma, cataract, macular degeneration and diabetic retinopathy. All can be treated with early detection.

1. Cataract.

Worldwide, cataract is the leading cause of blindness (nearly half the cases). The lens of the eye is composed of clear proteins but as you age these become more dense and less transparent. The density makes the lens harder, and less able to bend, reducing the ability to focus light onto the retina. The lack of transparency makes the lens cloudy, interfering with the images projected onto the retina. Cataracts can be surgically repaired (cataract implants). For children born with a cloudy lens, they can achieve normal vision if they receive this surgery before the age of six months. Without it, normal face recognition isn't possible.

Cataracts usually develop slowly, as the lens grows new layers of crystalline proteins. Either eye or both can be affected. There is no pain. People usually notice that colors are fading, they have trouble seeing at night, or that reading and recognizing faces is becoming more difficult.

2. Glaucoma.

Glaucoma is the second most common cause of blindness. It is caused by too much pressure in the aqueous humor of the eye. The aqueous humor (literally, watery fluid) is the space behind the cornea and in front of the lens. It is filled with a clear fluid which is constantly refreshed. New fluid is slowly released from the top of the eye and the old fluid is released through the Schlemm canals.

Like cataract, glaucoma is not painful. When the Schlemm canals get blocked, pressure inside the eye increases. Over time, this pressure damages the optic nerve resulting in a gradual loss of vision from the edges inward. The exception to the painless development is called closed-angle glaucoma. It can develop quickly, induce severe pain, and cause permanent loss of vision.

3. Macular Degeneration.

There are two types of macular degeneration. The most common is called nonexudative or dry macular degeneration. Yellow deposits, called drusen, grow between the retina and the blood supply behind it (choroid). The severity of the symptoms depends on the size of the drusen and how many there are. The result is a blurred spot in the middle of your visual field. This spot will gradually grow larger, eventually leaving you without clear vision. The center of your visual field is the part that you need to read, watch TV, and recognize faces.

Wet macular degeneration usually occurs more quickly. The blood vessels in the choroid exudate (seep out) between the choroid and the retina causing it to pull away. Dry macular generation can progress into wet macular degeneration. They are not mutually exclusive.

4. Diabetic Retinopathy.

Diabetes mellitus occurs when the body can't utilize glucose (Type II) or doesn't produce the necessary factors needed to utilize glucose (insulin). Insulin is a hormone which helps glucose get into cells, particularly those of muscles and the liver. If glucose isn't getting into cells where it can be used, it stays in the blood.

What's wrong with blood that is sweeter? High levels of glucose hurt the blood vessels by lowering the levels of vasodilators, such as nitric oxide. With less vasodilation, blood vessels narrow, blockages are more likely, and blood pressure increases (potentially harming the blood-brain barrier).

The retina has its own major blood supply called the choroid. The tiny vessels here can get clogged or rupture, causing blindness. People who have had diabetes for more than 20 years often acquire diabetic retinopathy.

93. Why Do We Sleep?

We sleep.

How long we sleep varies between species. In general, predators get more sleep than their prey. Lions get 18-20 hours of sleep but their meals (zebras and deer) only get a couple of hours, usually snoozing. Pythons, bats, armadillos and opossum get twice as much sleep as humans (~18 hrs. versus 8 hrs.). Elephants, sheep, cows, and goats get about half of the sleep we do. Clearly, we are not the best sleepers or the worst.

But why we sleep is unknown.

Although it is hard to tell about insects and fish, all birds and vertebrates sleep. Such a universal phenomenon must have a purpose. It must be important for all of us to do. But the truth is that why we sleep is still a mystery. We don't know, so we make up theories. Some of our theories are better than others.

Adaptive or inactivity theory suggests that sleep developed evolutionarily through natural selection for some unknown reason. The proponents suggest that laying still had an advantage but they don't know what that advantage was. Since we're pretty vulnerable while sleeping, it seems like a better evolutionary adaptation would be to sleep minimally, or at least be able to rotate hemispheres like dolphins do (alternate which hemisphere is asleep; no actual rotation occurs).

Energy conservation theory says we sleep so we can save up energy to gather, hunt or fight for food. But again, dolphins.

Restorative theory suggests that sleep does something for us. We use the time for body repair, and cleaning up the byproducts of internal combustion used in our neurons.

Brain plasticity theory notes that infants have lots of brain growth and lots of sleep. Maybe sleep fine-tunes the brain.

The least elegant but probably the truest theory is that the brain gets tired. The brain won't run smoothly after 24 hours. It stops utilizing glucose, even if there is plenty available.

In short, we sleep because we have to.

94. Why Do We Dream?

Dreams are sequences of images, sensations, and emotions, all mixed together. They occur involuntarily. You can't make yourself dream or stop yourself from dreaming (aside from waking up). Sometimes you can nudge them in one direction but they pretty much run on their own. Dreams can occur during any stage of sleep but are more common, longer and more vivid as the night progresses. If you remember a dream, it was probably the last one of the night.

Adult humans spend about 2 hours per night dreaming. The majority of our sleep is dreamless. People typically have 3-5 dreams per night. The first dreams are short but they get longer as the night progresses. Each dream occurs in real time. It takes as long to dream about walking across the room as it takes to actually walk across the room. Dreams aren't faster or slower than our awake activities.

Dreaming is increased and intensified during rapid eye movement (REM) sleep. As the night goes on, we have more REM sleep and more dreams. It appears that dreams are the result of REM sleep but it could be a spurious correlation. We don't know what causes dreams.

It is not clear if other animals dream but there is no reason to believe they don't. Most animals do have both REM and non-REM sleep. REM is a different experience from non-REM sleep. REM is similar to being awake. The brain doesn't show the synchronized waves of non-REM sleep. The brain is very active but the body is temporarily paralyzed. During REM, there is no release of any of the catecholamine neurotransmitters (including, dopamine, epinephrine, norepinephrine, serotonin, histamine, etc.). Although cows, horses and giraffes can stand during non-REM, they lie down for REM sleep.

There are four major dream theories. First, the ancient theory of dreams is that the fates and gods are talking to you. According to this view, the purpose of dreams is to provide creative thoughts or spiritual inspiration. Since opossums and armadillos sleep (and presumably dream) the most, it is difficult to say what the universe is trying to say.

Second, Freud's explanation of dreams is that unconscious wishes are being expressed. The sexual urges which are repressed by the conscious mind are freely released from the unconscious mind. Again, opossums and armadillos come to mind.

Third, Revonsuo's treat-simulation theory proposes that dreams help you plan and try out strategies you can use in real life. Did I mention the opossums and armadillos?

Fourth, Hobson & McCarley propose the activation theory of dreaming. Dreams are random neuron firings. They are like screen savers. While your brain restarts itself, images are randomly displayed. This version makes more sense when including the dreams of other animals. Armadillos aren't more in touch with the universe. Their screen savers run a lot longer than ours.

95. How Does What I Eat Affect My Brain Power?

Fortunately, not much, given our modern diet. Your brain doesn't really need artificial colors, "natural flavor", genetically modified proteins, polyunsaturated fats, high-fructose corn syrup, and additives you can't pronounce or spell. As a defense against our poor food selection habits, your stomach is filled with hydrochloric acid which demolishes everything it finds. The stuff that makes it through is bad for the rest of your body but it rarely makes it into the brain.

The digestive system converts everything into glucose. It takes longer for it to process proteins, sort of like burning large logs. It takes a relatively short time for it to process fats, sort of the twigs of our internal bonfire. It takes virtually no time to convert sugar into something that is useable.

The brain is more concerned about when you eat than what you eat. It doesn't like to be low on glucose. It likes a steady and reliable supply. The brain prefers you to eat regularly, get plenty of sleep, and exercise. It prefers you not using alcohol, not using caffeine, and not using drugs. As much as possible, keep your blood pressure under control, your weight within limits and your blood vessels free of debris.

There is some evidence that eating fish once a week is correlated with brain volume. But the connection is "ify." It works IF you bake or broil the fish (not if it is fried). It works IF you are physically active. It works IF your weight is under control. It works IF eating fish is part of your normal healthy lifestyle. Unfortunately, many of us are not able to be physically active, control our weight or eat as if we lived on a Mediterranean island. There is little you can do to combat disability, genetics and where you were born

Interestingly, eating fish more than once a week doesn't provide more help. Partly, this is because the major benefit is not from the omega-3 in the fish. The value of eating fish weekly is that it is a part of a lifestyle which includes weight control, physical activity, and being healthy.

Omega-3s are great for the heart and for general health. For most people, there is nothing you need to do to modify brain function. It is already doing the best it can.

It's not that omega-3s aren't good for your brain. In fact, the brain has its own source of omega acids (DHA). But there is some question about how much of omega-3 supplements actually cross the blood-brain barrier.

96. How Does Sugar Affect the Brain?

Your brain requires sugar. Specifically, it uses the simplest of sugars: glucose. Every neuron in your brain is a small internal combustion engine that uses glucose as its fuel. No glucose, no neural firings.

Since glucose is so important to our survival, we're very good at finding and consuming things that have glucose or can easily be converted into glucose. You'll recall that the body converts everything we eat into glucose. How long the conversion takes depends on what we've consumed. It takes a long time to process the proteins, a medium amount of time to convert fats and a short time to reduce simple carbohydrates into glucose.

Glucose is burned for its energy, which is measured in calories. A calorie is a unit of energy. Your local biology teacher probably demonstrated this by adding some liquid oxygen to a sample of food and setting a torch to it. The food will burn brightly like a little fire. That's what "burning" calories means.

Think of carbs, fats, and proteins as shipping containers of calories. They ship at different rates because of their different conversion rates. When the brain intakes glucose it takes note of what you did to achieve that and predicts how long it will be to the next shipment.

The brain uses several neurotransmitters to record the event. It uses dopamine to signal that something important has happened. The other neurotransmitters released when glucose arrives include serotonin (feeling of well-being), epinephrine (ready to do stuff) and norepinephrine (pay attention to this). The combination of these neurotransmitters makes you feel good. It's why we like eating.

97. Why Can't I Just Eat Carbs?

Let's assume chocolate cake is composed solely of carbohydrates. It, of course, also includes oil but let's pretend it's carbs only.

If the body only eats carbs, like a snack of chocolate cake, the brain notices the upsurge in glucose and marks the event as important, activating, soothing and attentive. It also reports pleasure. But after a bit of time, there is a sudden drop-off in supply which causes a "crash." The only choices are to eat more cake, find something else to eat or convert stored fat into glucose.

The brain doesn't like to reduce its stores of fat, just in case it's needed someday. It also isn't keen on eating something else because there will be a lag until the glucose arrives. So, if it has a choice, it will choose to eat more cake.

Alternatively, if you have a snack of cake and milk, the cake will be processed quickly but the crash will be avoided. The fat and protein in the milk will be converted and come to your rescue. The more milk and less cake, the less crash there will be. If the snack was a hot dog, tuna sandwich or chicken salad, there will be little or no crash.

Our problem isn't glucose. The problem is our supply of glucose. When we are out working in the fields and running away from saber-tooth tigers, the most available foods were nuts and berries. We did even better when we caught an occasional squirrel or salmon.

Now, it is not difficult to find food sources. There are plenty of options available. Unfortunately, the most packaged and easiest to carry options are naturally high in carbohydrates, plus they often contain extra amounts of sugar. The many names of extra sugar include dextrose, fructose, simple carbohydrates and synthesized sugars with names you can't pronounce. Even things you don't expect to contain sugar receive this supplemental boost.

Using glucose is a natural process that keeps us alive. An oversupply of sugar in your food source is the problem. Just because it is available doesn't mean you have to eat it. The reward system of your brain isn't going to help you here. You are going to have to pre-think your diet in order to make a change.

98. What Are Cognitive Maps?

Cognitive maps are mental representations of the real world. This is your ability to mentally find your way around a supermarket you frequently use. Visualizing the aisles or finding your way home are tasks which require input from the hippocampus. Without the hippocampus, we are unable to form new cognitive maps.

There appear to be two types of cognitive maps: sketch and bearing. Sketch maps use landmarks to find your way. "Go until you get to the big tree" is a sketch map. Using other people's sketch maps can be very confusing: "Go until you reach Darlington's farm, course it's not there anymore, but that's the spot you're looking for."

In contrast to the landmarks of sketch cognitive maps, bearing maps are vector-based. These are the kind of driving directions your phone gives you: "drive straight for 2.1 miles, turn left, drive 157 feet and turn right." They don't tell you that there is a big tree in 2.1 miles. They don't give you a sense of your surroundings. They provide the bare essentials.

People differ in their preference for one style of cognitive map but there don't seem to be any gender differences or actual performance differences. We are less confident or more comfortable using either landmarks or vectors but we seem equally able to produce both.

99. How Do Drugs Affect the Brain?

Drugs impact the brain at a synaptic level. They make connections between neurons last shorter, longer or occur? at weird intervals. Drugs impact the binding of neurotransmitters to receptors. They impact the unbinding process, the cleanup process and the reabsorption systems.

At a broader level, drugs impact which portions of the brain operate normally and which don't. Alcohol, for example, decreases brain activity overall. But it also shuts down the cerebellum first, which makes coordination of your hands and legs difficult to do. The sobriety tests given on site by the police are neurological tests used to diagnose problems in the cerebellum. Repeated use or binge drinking damages the amygdala, the hippocampus and the prefrontal cortex. Being a partier blunts your emotional response to normal social interaction.

Drugs also impact the brain's reward system. The euphoric high from a drug is the result of stimulating the release of epinephrine, norepinephrine, and dopamine. These neurotransmitters are used by the body to signal excitement, attention and importance/reward. Usually, when we achieve a goal or are given a compliment, our brain marks the event with a little burst of these neurotransmitters. When we experience an orgasm, there is a much larger dose. Think of cocaine and amphetamines as delivering a dose 1000 times stronger than your best sexual experience. Drugs are very rewarding; unnaturally so.

By delivering such a massive dose of euphoria, drugs hijack the reward system. Nothing seems as rewarding. All other experiences are blocked out. Losing your job, your family, and your self-respect seem like small prices to pay for reaching that high again.

Ironically, it is impossible to reach the same high again. The body automatically adjusts itself. If winning a major race is the highest high a person has ever experienced, the brain marks it as being #1 and everything else as being lower on the scale. When the first drug intake is experienced, it now becomes #1 and everything else is lower.

Notice that the brain doesn't rate experiences on an absolute basis. Every experience is rated in relative terms. We track if something is higher or lower but not by how much. Number 1 is top. But number 2, 3 and 39 are remarkably close. When drugs become king, everything else in life is unimportant.

100. Do Humans Have the Best Visual System?

We have the best system for us. We have two visual systems: one for day and one for night. Our daytime (photopic) system produces a continuous stream of sharp color pictures. It is our high-def video system. It is great for identifying people, objects and places. The images of a hawk are 3-4 time sharper but their stare is fixed. We have sharp images that are always in motion, always looking out for predators or new opportunities. And our vision is adjustable. We don't have the bifocal vision of horses but we can easily and quickly change focus. And we see in full color.

Color is important for finding foods you can eat. As omnivores (we'll eat anything), we need a visual system that allows us to see a wide range of colors so we can identify levels of ripeness, seasonal changes and tasty critters.

Our nighttime (scotopic) system produces a continuous stream of semi-sharp pictures. The images are a bit blurry but they need very little light to activate. They are great for detecting motion.

Human vision is not the best in every class. It is not as good in all areas as the specialized systems of other animals. But it is a good system for adaptive generalists.

101. What Are Humans Really Good At?

Humans are not the best at most things. We are not the tallest (elephants), fastest (cheetah) or heaviest (whale). We don't see as well as hawks, don't have the bifocal vision of horses, and can't swivel our heads 270 degrees like owls.

A mouse can hear tones 5x higher. Catfish have 25x more taste buds. Beavers can hold their breath for 45 minutes. Elephants can hold 2 gallons of water in their trunk. Woodcocks can only fly 5 mph but they can still fly!

Our brains aren't the heaviest. We have a 3-pound brain, which is sort of small if compared to elephants (11 pounds) or sperm whales (18 pounds). We don't have the most neurons in our nervous system. Compared to a cat (780 million), we're doing good (86 billion). But we're still beat out by the African elephant (270 billion). In a brain-to-body-mass ratio, we still don't win. We have about the same ratio of brain to body mass as a mouse.

Our brains don't have the most neocortical neurons (but its closer). We have about 21 billion gray matter neurons, just shy of the pilot whale's 36 billion, but we're way ahead of most everyone else, including elephants (5.6 billion).

We do best in the encephalization quotient (EQ). This is the ratio of brain mass to a set reference brain in the same taxonomic group. If you use cats as a reference animal for mammals (and why wouldn't you), cats score 1: a perfect match with themselves. Dolphins, monkeys and apes come in at about 5.0 (five times bigger-brained than a cat). We top the chart at 7.5.

Ultimately, it is not the size of the brain that matters. It is what you do with it. This is where we shine. What humans have is functionally. We have unmatched general processing power. Elephants use much of their large brains to control the temperature of their very large skins. We use our brains for a wide range of activities. We are generalists, not specialists.

Humans have some unique characteristics. We are great long-distance runners. A lion can run 50 mph but only for a few minutes, not for a whole hour. We only jog at 8 mph. but we can do so continuously for two or three days (until we drop dead from lack of sleep and water).

We are great at throwing things accurately. We are best within a 20-foot radius but we are capable of throwing and hitting someone 100-feet away with a stone. Skilled baseball pitchers can throw a ball 100 miles per hour.

We are great thinkers. We have a left hemisphere which allows us to explain to ourselves what happened in the past, what is going on now and what will probably happen in the future. The ability to storytell our experiences is astonishing.

We are great communicators. Not only can we explain life situations to ourselves, we can communicate with each other. We are terrific at language. We talk, present and write books. When was the last time you read a good book written by a dolphin?

PUTTING IT ALL TOGETHER

We've covered a great deal of material but there is still more to know. If you're looking to learn more about how the mind and body interacts, I have a website devoted to biological psychology. Just go to www.biologicalpsych.com. There are posts, lectures, videos, notes, quizzes and everything else I could think to add. If you can't find what you want, let me know and I'll look into providing it for you.

Ken Tangen

ABOUT THE AUTHOR

I have studied psychology most of my life. After receiving a B.A in psychology, I got a M.S. in counseling psychology, including all the course work for a masters in experimental psychology. After working a few years, I earned a PhD in a combination of cognition, measurement, education and psychology. I also did internships in counseling and family therapy.

I am a fanatic about teaching. It is my hobby, my love and my calling. I work hard at making complex things seem simple, or at least understandable. Writing is just another way of teaching.

Of course, you get to decide how successful I have been at my job. Feel free to send me your thoughts and comments. If you have positive things to say, email me: ken@kentangen.com. If you have negative things to say, call your mother.

BONUS

Free Course

I've created a free 5-day email course on breaking habits. Go to: www.kentangen.com/breaking and sign up.

www.ingramcontent.com/pod-product-compliance
Lightning Source LLC
Chambersburg PA
CBHW070125260726
48658CB00001B/266